365

ONE-MINUTE MEDITATIONS

GOD IS IN THE SMALL STUFF

FROM THE BESTSELLING SERIES BY BRUCE & STAN

BARBOUR
PUBLISHING

Published by Barbour Publishing, Inc., P.O. Box 719, Uhrichsville, Ohio 44683, www.barbourbooks.com

Our mission is to publish and distribute inspirational products offering exceptional value and biblical encouragement to the masses.

 Member of the
Evangelical Christian
Publishers Association

Printed in China.

A MINUTE A DAY CAN CHANGE YOUR LIFE.

We're all busy and pressed for time. But somewhere in our daily schedule, there must be at least sixty free seconds.

Look for that open minute and fill it with this book. *365 One-Minute Meditations from "God Is in the Small Stuff" Journal* provides a quick but powerful reading for every day of the year, promising real spiritual impact. Each day's entry features a carefully selected verse from God's Word, along with a condensed reading from the bestselling God Is in the Small Stuff series, with lines for journaling what's on your heart.

First released in 1998, *God Is in the Small Stuff* has encouraged hundreds of thousands of readers with its message of God's care and concern for each one of us—not only in the big issues of life, but in the ordinary, day-to-day details as well. This book is drawn from Bruce and Stan's daily devotional follow-up, *Keeping God in the Small Stuff*.

If you're seeking a spiritual lift, try *365 One-Minute Meditations from "God Is in the Small Stuff" Journal.* You'll only need a moment per day—but the benefits could be life-changing.

God Is in the Small Stuff

*M*any people treat the small stuff in life as if no one—not even God—has any control over what happens. If you're like most people, you tend to ask for God's involvement only in times of major need or crisis, and you miss out on the joy of watching God work in the small stuff of your life. God is in the big events, but He delights in working in the details.

Do not despise these small beginnings,
for the LORD rejoices to see the work begin.
ZECHARIAH 4:10

Use for the Purpose Intended

*Y*ou would laugh if someone expressed belief in a rabbit's foot dangling from his key chain. Sadly, some of us relegate our Bible to the status of "good-luck charm." Somehow we get a warm, fuzzy feeling just knowing that it is propped up in the bookshelf or lying on the nightstand. But we never read it. Only if it is opened, read, and studied can you access all of God's wisdom that the Bible contains. Move it off the shelf and into your heart.

For these commands and this teaching
are a lamp to light the way ahead of you.
PROVERBS 6:23

IN THE BEGINNING

January 3

*U*nless we know where our world came from, we don't know where it's going. That's why there's such a huge debate about how the universe began. There are only two options when it comes to the beginning of the universe. The first option is that a personal, intelligent, all-powerful, all-knowing, self-existent Creator made the heavens and the earth. The second option is that everything in the universe came from nothing. There is no third or fourth option. Either God made everything or He didn't.

In the beginning God created the heavens and the earth.
GENESIS 1:1 NIV

January 4

CONDUCT

*L*iving a godly life may make you different. You may find that your conduct pleases God but offends your friends, or vice versa. Jesus gave the analogy of "light" to show the importance of conduct. God wants you to shine into the darkness, not for your own publicity, but to bring credit to God. A candle doesn't do any good under a bowl. So go forward today being a light in your world.

"You are the light of the world. . . . Let your good deeds shine out for all to see,
so that everyone will praise your heavenly Father."
MATTHEW 5:14, 16

You Can't Prove God Exists

Sometimes we think we can prove God exists, but it just can't be done. You can't stick God under a microscope or view Him through a telescope, because God is a Spirit. No one has actually seen God (John 1:18). We know He exists because we can see the perfect order of the universe. We can feel His presence in our hearts. And we see the evidence of God's involvement in the world and in every detail of our lives.

They can clearly see his invisible qualities—
his eternal power and divine nature.
ROMANS 1:20

_____

_____

_____

_____

_____

What It Takes

The coach of any athletic team will tell you that you have to practice if you want to win. In the spiritual realm, "winning" is getting to know God and having our lives transformed in the process. As you are diligent in pursuing God, you'll notice gradual changes in your life. You are working for a goal that is worthy of your best efforts.

I strain to reach the end of the race and receive the prize for which God,
through Christ Jesus, is calling us up to heaven.
PHILIPPIANS 3:14

_____

_____

_____

_____

_____

THERE'S NOTHING YOU CAN DO

January 7

*I*n the physical world, there are many ways to be saved, but first you have to be in a situation in which you would eventually die without help. The same principle applies in the spiritual world. All of our efforts won't help us spiritually, but God is willing to save us—if we will only believe in Him.

God saved you by his special favor when you believed.
And you can't take credit for this; it is a gift from God.
EPHESIANS 2:8

_____

_____

_____

_____

_____

January 8

CONFIDENCE

*T*here is a lot of talk these days about "building your self-esteem" so you will have confidence to make it in society. Instead of being confident in yourself, try placing your confidence in God, who will never fail you. If you belong to God, no one and nothing can separate you from His love and protection. This promise can give you real confidence.

I am convinced that nothing can ever separate us from his love. . . .
Our fears for today, our worries about tomorrow, and even the powers
of hell can't keep God's love away.
ROMANS 8:38

_____

_____

_____

_____

_____

Pleasing God

*I*t's only natural to want to please someone you like. You do it not because you're obligated but because you want to give joy to someone. God likes it when you please Him, but don't do it to give Him joy—God doesn't need to have His spirits lifted. Pleasing God is for your benefit. When you do the things and think the thoughts that please God, your life takes on new meaning and purpose.

> *We will receive whatever we request because we obey him*
> *and do the things that please him.*
> 1 JOHN 3:22

Be Content

*I*t is impossible to weigh your contentment on a scale of stuff. If stuff is your measurement, you will never have enough because there will always be someone who has more stuff than you do. Stuff has nothing to do with contentment, because contentment is a matter of your heart, not your wallet. Real contentment comes when you focus your heart and your mind on things above rather than things on earth (Colossians 3:2).

> *I know how to live on almost nothing or with everything.*
> *I have learned the secret of living in every situation.*
> PHILIPPIANS 4:12

LOOKING AT GOD INSTEAD OF YOUR CIRCUMSTANCES

January 11

*W*e make life a lot harder than it needs to be. This happens whenever the circumstances in our lives discourage us. It is in those tough times that God seems distant. Instead of trying to see God through your circumstances, take the opposite approach. Look at your circumstances through God's eyes. God doesn't see your circumstances as insurmountable. Stop worrying about your obstacles and start thinking about the God who can help you overcome them.

I can do everything with the help of Christ who gives me the strength I need.
PHILIPPIANS 4:13

January 12

THE INSIGNIFICANCE OF INSIGNIFICANCE

It doesn't take much effort to feel insignificant. Another person makes a negative comment about you, and it doesn't take long for you to believe that your work or your position doesn't count for much. That's no place for someone whom God loves and cares about more than can be imagined. Your life has value, and what you do has significance because you are important to God.

"Not even a sparrow, worth only half a penny, can fall to the ground without your Father knowing it. . . .
So don't be afraid; you are more valuable to him than a whole flock of sparrows."
MATTHEW 10:29, 31

It's Okay to Feel Small

The opposite of feeling insignificant is feeling self-important. There's only one problem with putting yourself at the center of the universe: You tend to push God out. You belong to God, who designed and built you as surely as He set the moon and the stars in place.

When I look at the night sky and see the work of your fingers—the moon and the stars you have set in place—
what are mortals that you should think of us, mere humans that you should care for us?
PSALM 8:3–4

_____

_____

_____

_____

_____

Ambition

Ambition is natural. After all, you want a happy family, strong friendships, financial security, and good health. Jesus taught about the great irony of self-ambition. He said you must lose your life in order to keep it. This paradox forces you to choose which is more important: your physical life or your eternal soul. Let God be your priority. Let living in His kingdom be your ambition.

"How do you benefit if you gain the whole world but lose or forfeit your own soul in the process?"
LUKE 9:25

_____

_____

_____

_____

_____

January 15

Do You Want to Know God's Will?

*O*ne of the mysteries of life is the will of God. While it's true that we'll never know all of God's will, we can know a lot of what He wants us to do by spending time with Him. So you could say that the only way to really know God's will is to really know God. How do you do that? By reading the Bible and by talking with Him as often as you can.

Your word is a lamp for my feet and a light for my path.
PSALM 119:105

_____

_____

_____

_____

_____

January 16

Are You God's "Fair-Weather" Friend?

*N*obody likes a fair-weather friend. Neither does God, but sadly, many of us treat Him that way. We give God our adoration and allegiance only when He fulfills our expectations. But when difficulties arise, we are quick to blame God. Aren't you glad that His love for us endures no matter how we treat Him? That is true love from a true friend, and that should be how we respond to Him.

We know how much God loves us, and we have put our trust in him.
1 JOHN 4:16

_____

_____

_____

_____

_____

Seek This First

*W*henever you set goals for yourself, it's important to prioritize them. As you get to know God better, you will find that He will ask you to operate at a higher level of living. That means you shouldn't worry about your short-term, personal needs. Trust God to provide for the everyday stuff, and then make God and His kingdom your highest priority.

> *"He will give you all you need from day to day if you live for him*
> *and make the Kingdom of God your primary concern."*
> MATTHEW 6:33

_____

_____

_____

_____

_____

Two Kinds of Anger

*T*here are two kinds of anger. There is "righteous" anger that comes out of a righteous response to sin. You can express this emotion and still have God in control of your life. The second kind of anger controls you. This is the kind of anger that the Bible warns against. Only God should have control of your life. Make sure that your temper is not pushing Him out of His rightful place.

> *Don't be quick-tempered, for anger is the friend of fools.*
> ECCLESIASTES 7:9

_____

_____

_____

_____

_____

KEEP A BALANCED PERSPECTIVE

January 19

*H*ave you ever noticed how poorly people treat each other? Is it because there's no other way to make ourselves feel better? No, we think it has more to do with God. The less time we spend learning to know God, the more time we have to criticize others. On the other hand, the more we invite God into the details of our lives, the more likely we will be to encourage other people rather than tear them down.

Live a life filled with love for others, following the example of Christ.
EPHESIANS 5:2

January 20

SIT STILL AND LISTEN

*P*rayer isn't talking to God. Prayer is really talking *with* God. Most of our prayers include a lot of our own talking, but they usually lack the important aspect of listening. Of course we don't mean to suggest that you are going to hear a celestial voice booming in the heavens. That's not how God works. You hear Him, not audibly with your ears, but internally in your heart and soul. You need to be quiet for a few moments so you can hear Him.

"Be silent, and know that I am God!"
PSALM 46:10

The Knife of God

There's a reason the Bible is the world's bestselling book and its message changes millions of lives every year. The Bible is God's Word. God knows your inner thoughts and has a message of love and hope just for you. The Bible will open you up so God can pour His words into you.

For the word of God is full of living power. It is sharper than the sharpest knife, cutting deep into our innermost thoughts and desires. It exposes us for what we really are.
HEBREWS 4:12

Faith

The problem with the world is not that people lack faith. The problem is that their faith is misplaced. Most people put their faith in things or in people who will someday prove unreliable and unfulfilling. God is the only unfailing place for your faith. He always makes good on His promises. Nothing and nobody else but God is worthy of your complete trust.

"Have faith in God. . . . All that's required is that you really believe and do not doubt in your heart."
MARK 11:22–23

TAKE GOD'S COMMANDS PERSONALLY

January 23

*H*ow we love the promises of God! But what about the commands of scripture? For some reason we tend to interpret a command as being more general in nature. Instead of personalizing it, we figure it applies to other people, especially those in full-time Christian service. Is it okay to take God's promises personally while applying His commands generally? All of God's Word is personal. All of it—the promises as well as the commands—applies to all of us.

You made me; you created me.
Now give me the sense to follow your commands.
PSALM 119:73

January 24

HOW CAN YOU HELP?

*T*he Bible tells us that we are to confront a friend if we notice some aspect of our friend's life that is contrary to the character of Christ. Maybe you're reluctant to mention a problem because your friend may feel the freedom to do the same to you. You should welcome that kind of confrontation, because it will help you stay close to God.

Dear brothers and sisters, if another Christian is overcome by some sin,
you who are godly should gently and humbly help that person back onto the right path.
GALATIANS 6:1

Be a Quick Listener

The most important part of communication is listening. Listen first; then talk. There are at least two benefits to this pattern. To start with, the only way to learn something is to listen. The main advantage of hearing others speak first is that you may realize that what you were about to say is completely wrong or meaningless. The other benefit is that you are less likely to get upset if you listen before you speak.

> *Be quick to listen, slow to speak, and slow to get angry.*
> JAMES 1:19

Conformity

There is tremendous pressure to conform to our culture. But have you noticed that the group mentality is usually wrong? Check your life to see if society is influencing your thinking. You probably haven't been brainwashed totally, but there is a strong chance that your thinking has been influenced. If you are going to be a fully devoted follower of God, you have to make sure that you don't conform to the culture in any significant way that would compromise godly principles.

> *Don't copy the behavior and customs of this world.*
> ROMANS 12:2

RENEW YOUR MIND

January 27

A lot of brilliant people have done some pretty stupid stuff. Our minds don't need more information to improve. Our minds need transformation. The only One who can enter our hearts and transform our minds is God. God must change our minds in every detail. You must invite Him to do His work, and "there must be a spiritual renewal of your thoughts and attitudes" (Ephesians 4:23).

But let God transform you into a new person by changing
the way you think.
ROMANS 12:2

January 28

DO WHAT IS GOOD

*E*very once in a while, we need to hear a great motivational sermon. But you must avoid becoming a motivational junkie. If you become dependent on motivational sermons, you'll fail in your spiritual life. Instead of depending on someone else to fire you up, get busy helping others. When "doing good" for others is a habit in your life, you'll find that it happens regardless of your emotions.

Don't get tired of doing what is good. Don't get discouraged and give up,
for we will reap a harvest of blessing at the appropriate time.
GALATIANS 6:9

Control Your Anger

*N*o emotion ignites more quickly than anger. And once it's out there, it's hard to put a cork on your anger. The Bible instructs us to be slow to anger. It doesn't say we shouldn't get angry. We're human. We get angry. But when we are thoughtful and patient, hearing others out before making our pronouncements, we are less likely to be foolish or destructive in our anger. Here's another reason to manage our anger: God is pleased when we keep our anger under control.

> *Your anger can never make things right in God's sight.*
> JAMES 1:20

Joy

*T*hink about being in the presence of the most loving person you know. Are you jealous that the disciples got to know Jesus personally? Well, don't be. You can't presently experience the joy of seeing Him face-to-face, but that day will come. And in the meantime, you'll have the joy that comes from having a personal relationship with the almighty God.

> *"Truly, you will weep and mourn over what is going to happen to me,*
> *but the world will rejoice. You will grieve, but your grief will suddenly*
> *turn to wonderful joy when you see me again."*
> JOHN 16:20

CHURCH DIFFERENCES

January 31

*D*rive around any town and you'll see a lot of different churches. It's fine that we have different churches with different names and different ways of doing things. Differences are good! It shows that the universal Church, composed of all believers everywhere, is a diverse bunch. But we should never let our differences separate us. God sees no distinction between men and women, rich and poor, slave and free, Baptist and Catholic.

This is the church of the living God, which is the pillar and support of the truth.
1 TIMOTHY 3:15

_____

_____

_____

_____

February 1

LOVE BEFORE FIRST SIGHT

*G*od didn't love you at first sight, because He actually loved you long before you were born. In fact, He loved you before He created the world. Don't ever think that God loves you because you have decided to love Him. Your love definitely pleases Him, but He is not reciprocating your affection. God has been loving you and awaiting your affection throughout history. Now that's a love story.

Long ago, even before he made the world, God loved us and chose us in Christ to be holy and without fault in his eyes.
EPHESIANS 1:4

_____

_____

_____

_____

GOD'S WHISPER

*T*here are times when God speaks through other people in order to tell us something. And sometimes God will speak directly to us. If you want to hear God's voice, the first thing you need to be is quiet. God won't shout above the cacophony of your life. God will come to you in a gentle whisper—in your thoughts and in your heart. But you'll never hear God's voice unless you turn off the noise.

And after the fire there was the sound of a gentle whisper.
1 KINGS 19:12

_____

_____

_____

_____

_____

GOSSIP

*G*ossip and laziness are closely related. Christians can get a bad reputation by being lazy gossips. Do you want to improve the perception of Christians and bring honor to God in the process? Then work hard, keep to your own business, and never get tired of doing good.

We hear that some of you are living idle lives, refusing to work and wasting time meddling in other people's business. In the name of the Lord Jesus Christ, we appeal to such people—no, we command them: Settle down and get to work.
2 THESSALONIANS 3:11–12

_____

_____

_____

_____

MAKE YOUR PRAYERS A PRIORITY

A lot of people pray, but few people pray effectively. If you pray only when you're in trouble, you're not praying effectively. Praying when you're exhausted and barely able to keep your eyes open is not effective. Effective prayer doesn't just happen; it takes effort, devotion, and discipline. Think of prayer like a muscle—the more you exercise it, the stronger it will get.

Devote yourselves to prayer with an alert mind and a thankful heart.
COLOSSIANS 4:2

DO YOU LOVE GOD?

D o you love God? Love means more than just knowing or respecting Him. Are you giving Him a place of priority in your life above everything else? Are you only interested in the parts of Him that you want (such as His forgiving nature)? Or do you love God for all His attributes (such as His holiness that abhors sinful behavior)? Spend this day considering the question, "Do you love God?"

" 'You must love the Lord your God with all your heart, all your soul, all your mind, and all your strength.' "
MARK 12:30

PREACHERS CAN'T DO IT ALONE

*W*e believe the vast majority of preachers prepare and deliver their sermons for one overarching purpose—so those of us sitting in the pews might be motivated to live our lives more for God and less for ourselves. Of course the preachers can't do it alone, no matter how powerful their sermons. We are the Church, and wherever we go, we take the sermons—and all that they mean—with us.

> *Wherever we go he uses us to tell others about the Lord and to spread the Good News like a sweet perfume.*
> 2 CORINTHIANS 2:14

OVERCOME YOUR FEARS

*P*eople fear tangible things such as being injured, robbed, or cheated. They also fear intangible things like being rejected, experiencing failure, or giving a speech. Fear can keep you from doing the right thing at the right time. If you want to overcome your fears, you must have faith that God can conquer them.

> *When he woke up, he rebuked the wind and said to the water, "Quiet down!" Suddenly the wind stopped, and there was a great calm. And he asked them, "Why are you so afraid? Do you still not have faith in me?"*
> MARK 4:39–40

SIGNED BY THE ARTIST

The human body is the most complex organism in the universe. You can choose to believe that your amazing body evolved from a slimy swamp creature, but isn't it more logical to believe that an extremely intelligent and powerful Creator designed your body and your mind? Just as an artist signs his work, God has left His imprint on your life. And it's that imprint that gives your life meaning.

God created people in his own image; God patterned them after himself; male and female he created them.
GENESIS 1:27

_____

_____

_____

_____

_____

NEEDING GOD WHEN YOU THINK YOU DON'T

You are in real danger the moment you think that you are independent and self-sufficient. If you get to that stage, you are likely to stop relying on God. When that happens, we start making decisions and choices based on our own faulty wisdom instead of God's divine direction. If things are going well for you, give praise to God for your present situation. Realize that God (not you) is the One who is responsible for creating those tranquil circumstances in your life.

Pride goes before destruction, and haughtiness before a fall.
PROVERBS 16:18

_____

_____

_____

_____

_____

The Passing of Time

Time is God's gift to us. It's a way to measure and celebrate the events of our lives as they unfold. In that sense, time gives us joy. Time also provides a way for us to anticipate things to come. In that sense, time gives us hope. Time can also give us anxiety. There is never a time when we can't turn to God and ask for His involvement in our circumstances.

God has made everything beautiful for its own time.
ECCLESIASTES 3:11

_____

_____

_____

_____

_____

Eternity Is in Your Heart

Have you ever wondered why you think about forever? The reason the ideas of "forever" and "ever after" permeate your thinking is that God put them there. He stuck those thoughts in your head and your heart because He wants you to know that He exists, even though you can't see Him. God also wants you to know that He dwells in a place far beyond the universe He created. It's a place called heaven.

God. . .has planted eternity in the human heart.
ECCLESIASTES 3:11

_____

_____

_____

_____

Our View Is Limited

February 12

There's so much about God that we don't know, and rather than being patient and waiting for Him to give us the right information at the appropriate time, we conclude that He either doesn't care about us or isn't able to help us. Both of these conclusions are dead wrong. The only way to avoid these frustrating conclusions is to concentrate on what we do know about God and trust Him for the rest.

People cannot see the whole scope of God's work from beginning to end.
ECCLESIASTES 3:11

February 13

Sorrow

There is a fine line between sorrow and guilt. God wants you to be sorry when you have done something wrong. Sincere sorrow is part of the process of repentance. Satan, on the other hand, wants you to go far beyond sorrow. He uses guilt as an oppressive emotion. The next time you regret your actions, thank God. Your sorrow is a sign that Jesus is alive and active in your life.

God can use sorrow in our lives to help us turn away from sin and seek salvation. We will never regret that kind of sorrow.
2 CORINTHIANS 7:10

THE REALITY OF ETERNITY

*G*od created you so you could live forever. There's only one problem. Sin got in the way. Unless you deal with the sin problem, you'll never live to see forever with God. But there's a way to deal with the sin problem. When you accept "the free gift of God. . .eternal life through Christ Jesus our Lord" (Romans 6:23), God puts you back on track for forever with Him.

> *"Don't be afraid! I am the First and the Last. I am the living one who died. Look,*
> *I am alive forever and ever! And I hold the keys of death and the grave."*
> REVELATION 1:17–18

_____

_____

_____

_____

_____

WHO IS GOD?

*S*ome people form their beliefs about God based on their personal opinions. God isn't going to change His character to conform to what we think about Him. God is who He is. Our understanding and beliefs about God should be based on what we learn about Him from the Bible. Make sure your concept of who God is conforms to what God says about Himself.

> *"Let them boast in this alone: that they truly know me and understand that I am the LORD*
> *who is just and righteous, whose love is unfailing, and that I delight in these things."*
> JEREMIAH 9:24

_____

_____

_____

_____

_____

CHARACTER COUNTS

*S*ome people believe it's possible for a person to possess both a public and a private character, even if the two are very different. Character is defined by integrity, and at the heart of integrity is the idea of wholeness. One of the best ways to keep your life whole is to pay attention to the small stuff. Do what it takes every day to develop your character and preserve your integrity. Don't live your life to please others. Live your life to please God.

May integrity and honesty protect me, for I put my hope in you.
PSALM 25:21

SECURITY

*M*any people look to their own financial resources for their security. How should you maintain the proper balance? Here's a simple test. If your treasure is money, you will be plagued with anxieties about losing it every time the NASDAQ takes a tumble. On the other hand, if your real treasure is your relationship with God, the focus of your life will be on Him. Put your treasure in the kingdom of God, which will last forever.

"Yes, a person is a fool to store up earthly wealth but not have a rich relationship with God."
LUKE 12:21

LIFE IS A MARATHON

*W*hy do bad things happen to you? There are times when you just don't know. Other times, you know exactly why difficult stuff is happening. Either way, you need to believe that the end results will be for your own good. Remember that life is a marathon, not a sprint. The pain you are feeling today is just part of the overall race, and the prize is guaranteed if you cross the finish line.

God blesses the people who patiently endure testing. Afterward they will
receive the crown of life that God has promised to those who love him.
JAMES 1:12

_____

_____

_____

_____

_____

BUSYNESS

*T*here is a principle of economics: If you lose money on every sale, you can't make up for it in quantity. Some people need to apply this principle to the activities of their lives. They mistakenly think that increasing their commitments is admirable because "more is better." But sometimes more is worse, and this is particularly true of activities in our daily schedule. Before you get busier than you already are, evaluate what you are doing. Maybe you should delete some commitments from your schedule so that you can do a better job with fewer activities.

Whatever you do, do well.
ECCLESIASTES 9:10

_____

_____

_____

_____

DESTRUCTIVE CRITICISM

February 20

*W*hereas constructive criticism can be helpful to others, most criticism is quite destructive. Destructive criticism takes the attention away from the person doing the criticizing. It is motivated by fear—fear of being criticized or fear of having to be honest. It comes out of a heart where love is momentarily lacking. Love is actually the antidote to destructive criticism. When you are motivated by love, you are less likely to be critical of others, because you'll have their best interests in mind.

Such love has no fear because perfect love expels all fear.
1 JOHN 4:18

February 21

CREATION

*T*here may be legitimate questions about the "when" and the "how" of creation, but there is no doubt about "who" created all things. The Bible says God created our universe (Genesis 1:1). But the Bible clarifies that Christ had a primary role in the creation of the world. He was the intelligent designer in the whole process. When you contemplate the enormity of the universe or the intricacies of nature, remember who is responsible for them.

Christ is the one through whom God created everything in heaven and earth. . . .
He existed before everything else began, and he holds all creation together.
COLOSSIANS 1:16–17

LISTEN AND LEARN

*G*od sends others to help you grow as a Christian. First, He sends the Holy Spirit. God also sends people to teach you His truth and to come alongside you as your spiritual friends and mentors. God has equipped them to feed you spiritual food so you can grow. You need to listen and learn.

> *You must remain faithful to the things you have been taught.*
> *You know they are true, for you know you can trust those who taught you.*
> 2 TIMOTHY 3:14

_____

_____

_____

_____

_____

LISTENING FOR GOD'S VOICE

February 23

*I*f we expect to hear God only in the spectacular moments, we will miss most of what He is trying to say. Our lives are filled with common circumstances. Because God wants to be in constant communication with us, He talks during those times, as well. Try listening for Him in the ordinary routine of your life, and you'll be surprised at how much He wants to tell you.

> *"Anyone who is willing to hear should listen and understand! And be sure to pay*
> *attention to what you hear. The more you do this, the more you will understand."*
> MARK 4:23–24

_____

_____

_____

_____

_____

FAMILY NAMES

The main reason we don't take more pride in our family names is that we don't know our family heritage. It doesn't take much to dig up some information on your family name. When it comes to both the heritage and the meaning of your name, you can either ignore them or live up to them. And if there isn't much to live up to, then determine to bring honor to your family name.

A good name is more desirable than great riches.
PROVERBS 22:1 NIV

_____

_____

_____

_____

_____

HYPOCRISY

When Jesus was on earth, there were no bigger phonies than the religious leaders (the scribes and Pharisees). Jesus called them hypocrites because they bragged about their extreme habits of cleanliness, but internally, where it mattered, their motives were evil and filthy. Centuries later, many of us are acting like the scribes and Pharisees. We put on a good show on the outside, but our thoughts and attitudes are not pleasing to God.

"You try to look like upright people outwardly, but inside your hearts are filled with hypocrisy and lawlessness."
MATTHEW 23:28

_____

_____

_____

_____

_____

WHO IS JESUS?

*J*esus is God's Son, completely perfect yet able to identify with our weaknesses. Jesus is the most extraordinary person ever to live on earth, and God has raised Him up to the heights of heaven, where He is worthy of the highest praise that heaven and earth can deliver.

> *The Son reflects God's own glory, and everything about him represents God exactly.*
> *He sustains the universe by the mighty power of his command.*
> HEBREWS 1:3

GRAB THE TOWEL

February 27

*R*emember the story of Jesus washing the feet of the disciples? What makes this incident so ironic is that the disciples had been arguing earlier about which of them was going to be "greatest" in God's kingdom. We can't be too critical of the disciples, because we make the same mistake. We're so eager to be important, to be noticed, and to have prestige. Let Jesus be your example. Forget about your own self-importance and focus on the needs of others.

> *"The greatest among you must be a servant."*
> MATTHEW 23:11

STAY AT IT EVERY DAY

Knowing God doesn't happen overnight; it takes a lifetime. And it starts with one small task (such as reading the Bible for fifteen minutes each day) repeated over and over again. Remember that the heart of discipline is repetition, not completion. Have a goal in mind— such as knowing God better—so that your daily routine of discipline takes on meaning.

Without wavering, let us hold tightly to the hope we say we have,
for God can be trusted to keep his promise.
HEBREWS 10:23

FREEDOM FROM SIN

Before you belonged to God, you were entrapped by your sin nature. But with your salvation, you were freed not only from sin's eternal death penalty but also from the snare of sin. You are really free to choose godly living in every situation.

Thank God! Once you were slaves of sin. . . . But now you are free from the power of sin
and have become slaves of God. Now you do those things that lead to holiness and result in eternal life.
ROMANS 6:17, 22

STRETCH YOURSELF

If you reach every goal you set, you aren't setting the right kind of goals. Reaching goals takes time, and some goals require a lifetime to reach. If you've never set a goal that brings fear into your heart, you are missing out on one of the great joys of life. A terrifying goal doesn't have to be dangerous. But it should stretch you so far that you wonder how you will ever reach it.

So we make it our goal to please him.
2 CORINTHIANS 5:9 NIV

_____

_____

_____

_____

_____

NO RELIGION NECESSARY

If your religion is just a bunch of dos and don'ts, then God isn't interested in it. God wants your genuine faith, not your meaningless rituals. He wants you to respond to Him out of love, not out of compulsion or guilt or habit. He wants you to enjoy the freedom of faith without dreading rigid rules.

"You will know the truth, and the truth will set you free."
JOHN 8:32

_____

_____

_____

_____

_____

THE ROLE OF GOVERNMENT

March 3

*I*t's very easy to blur the lines between our faith and our politics, but nowhere in scripture does God tell us to support only those people who agree with our theological positions. God tells us to submit to those in authority, obey them, and pray for them. Just as we trust God to rule in our hearts, we need to trust Him by obeying those who rule over us, even if we disagree.

Remind your people to submit to the government and its officers.
They should be obedient, always ready to do what is good.
TITUS 3:1

_____

_____

_____

_____

_____

March 4

DOUBT

*Y*ou wouldn't think that wisdom and doubt are opposites, but they are. To have doubt is to be unsettled, like a wave driven by the wind. Wisdom involves trusting someone who not only has more experience than you do but also has your best interests in mind. When you have doubts, you can go to God for the answers.

But when you ask him, be sure that you really expect him to answer,
for a doubtful mind is as unsettled as a wave of the sea that is driven and tossed by the wind.
JAMES 1:6

_____

_____

_____

_____

_____

Your Body and Your Mind

*D*id you know that there is a direct relationship between your physical fitness and your spiritual life? If your body is run-down because of the choices you make—such as eating poorly or never getting enough sleep—then your mind won't be at its sharpest. God wants you to have a healthy body so you can have a healthy mind, because a healthy mind enables you to love God even more.

God bought you with a high price. So you must honor God with your body.
1 CORINTHIANS 6:20

Little Things

*I*t is only natural that you want to do great things for God. You want to prove how much you love Him by doing something great and glorious for Him. Just be faithful with the seemingly small things in your life. Loving your family, being kind to a stranger, helping a neighbor—these are small things that have great significance in God's eyes.

"And the King will tell them, 'I assure you, when you did it to one of
the least of these my brothers and sisters, you were doing it to me!'"
MATTHEW 25:40

BEST FRIENDS

March 7

*N*one of us is above the objective, truthful, and loving correction of someone who has our best interests in mind. This is where your friends come in. Your best friends will level with you, even at the risk of alienating you for a while. They'll tell you privately where you're wrong and where you need to straighten up, as long as you let them know ahead of time that you want the truth.

"I am warning you! If another believer sins, rebuke him; then if he repents, forgive him."
LUKE 17:3

_____
_____
_____
_____
_____

March 8

KINDNESS

*J*esus established the standard for kindness when He said, "Love your neighbor as yourself" (Luke 10:27). This principle can give you a quick and easy test to determine whether you are showing kindness to others. In any situation, you can just ask yourself, "How would I like to be treated?"

"Now which of these three would you say was a neighbor to the man who was attacked by bandits?" Jesus asked.
The man replied, "The one who showed him mercy." Then Jesus said, "Yes, now go and do the same."
LUKE 10:36–37

_____
_____
_____
_____
_____

INTEGRITY IS SOMETHING YOU ARE

*T*he mind is a powerful thing. Not only do you act upon what you think about, but you also become what you think about. Take the matter of integrity. Integrity is not something you do; it's something you are. How do you become a person of integrity? You must first think about the things that define integrity. When you occupy your mind with the right things, you will do the right things. You can count on that.

Fix your thoughts on what is true and honorable and right.
PHILIPPIANS 4:8

PICTURE THIS

*I*n your mind you can picture things of purity and beauty, whether you've actually seen them or just read about them in a book. By using your imagination, you can bring beautiful objects and places into your head. Be aware of the beauty and detail of God's creation. Read God's Word daily. The more beauty you see or read about with your eyes, the more beauty you will hold in your mind.

Think about things that are pure and lovely and admirable.
PHILIPPIANS 4:8

DO YOUR PART;
LET GOD DO HIS

March 11

We want to accomplish wonderful things for God before we have prepared ourselves. Instead of worrying about what we can do for God, we should be concerned with getting to know Him better. We don't have to postpone sharing our faith with others until we have obtained an advanced degree in theology. But as we gain a deeper understanding of who He is, then He will open the doors for us to serve Him.

Jesus called out to them, "Come, be my disciples,
and I will show you how to fish for people!"
MATTHEW 4:19

March 12

GOD GETS THE CREDIT

When you look at an object of beauty—say, a beautiful painting—do you give credit to the painting for its beauty? The credit goes to the artist, who painted this thing of beauty. The artist deserves your admiration because the artist is worthy. The same goes for God, the great Artist who created the earth. He's the One who is worthy of praise, not the creation.

They worshiped the things God made but not the Creator himself, who is to be praised forever. Amen.
ROMANS 1:25

Think about Heaven

*N*o image is worthier of your imagination than heaven. We all think about heaven from time to time, but too often we limit our imagination to streets of gold (Revelation 21:21) and "mansions" (John 14:2 KJV). Heaven will be much more than we have ever seen or could ever imagine (1 Corinthians 2:9). When you fill your mind with the infinite possibilities of heaven, you have no choice but to think about God.

> *Let heaven fill your thoughts. Do not think only about things down here on earth.*
> COLOSSIANS 3:2

Captive Thoughts

*I*f our thoughts were printed out for all to read, we would be pretty embarrassed. It's those little wanderings into the dark corners of our hearts and minds that are the constant problem. That's why we need to ask God to control our thoughts, which He will do through the Holy Spirit, who will teach us and remind us of everything God has told us (John 14:26).

> *We take captive every thought to make it obedient to Christ.*
> 2 CORINTHIANS 10:5 NIV

INTEGRITY

March 15

*Y*ou know you shouldn't lie, but there are many circumstances in life when the truth may seem irrelevant. Is absolute honesty required at all times? Jesus taught that integrity and truth have only one level (Matthew 5:33–37). Your word should be enough. Jesus wants your words to be truthful in every conversation.

Most of all, my brothers and sisters, never take an oath, by heaven or earth or anything else. Just say a simple yes or no.
JAMES 5:12

_____

_____

_____

_____

March 16

KNOWING GOD

*S*piritual growth is not a matter of trying harder. The spiritual disciplines of prayer and Bible reading are part of the training process. Don't view them as daily chores that must be endured. Consider them as an opportunity that allows you to come closer into God's presence and dialogue with Him. There is no greater reward than knowing God. He is worth your effort.

Jesus replied, "Your problem is that you don't know the Scriptures, and you don't know the power of God."
MARK 12:24

_____

_____

_____

_____

_____

JESUS' AUTHORITY

*W*hen people heard Jesus teach, they were amazed. Jesus spoke with authority because He knew the scriptures. People could see from the actions of His life that He believed what He taught. Can you communicate the truth about God in a way that makes it exciting and appealing to others? Your answer to this question will depend on how much you know, and believe, about God.

> *They were amazed at his teaching, for he taught as one who had real authority—quite unlike the teachers of religious law.*
> **MARK 1:22**

_____

_____

_____

_____

_____

WHAT WOULD JESUS DO?

*T*he greatest person who ever walked the earth was Jesus. Yet Jesus is more than a person, and His life is more than a story. Jesus is God with skin on, the Creator of the universe in human form. Jesus experienced all of our temptations and human frailties, yet He lived a perfect life. That's why we can look to Jesus as our example for living.

> *Those who say they live in God should live their lives as Christ did.*
> **1 JOHN 2:6**

_____

_____

_____

_____

_____

Passion and Compassion

March 19

God doesn't want us to ignore the "real world." He wants us to bring a spiritual dimension into it. You have only to examine the life of Jesus to realize that God doesn't want us isolated in some monastery (or the church sanctuary). Jesus walked the streets and met the people. He was moved with compassion and responded to the needs of the people. Worship God today by connecting with the people around you.

The unfailing love of the Lord never ends! By his mercies we have been kept from complete destruction.
LAMENTATIONS 3:22

_____

_____

_____

_____

_____

March 20

Don't Neglect Your Life

There's a great principle that is seen in the natural world. It's called the law of entropy: Over time, things naturally lose energy, decay, or move from order to disorder. Let's focus on some of the intangible things like character and integrity. If you leave these areas alone and fail to give them attention, they will lose energy, decay, and move from order to disorder. Anything that requires your time and energy—such as your relationship with God—will go backward if you neglect it.

You must warn each other every day. . .so that none of you will be deceived by sin.
HEBREWS 3:13

_____

_____

_____

_____

_____

Your Love

*W*e love when we feel like it, and that includes loving God. Yet we are commanded to love God. In fact, loving God is the most important instruction that Jesus ever gave (Mark 12:29–30). You should commit yourself to it completely: with your heart (feelings), your soul (spirit), your mind (intellect), and your strength (action). Loving God is a lifelong process that involves the entire being.

This is real love. It is not that we loved God, but that he loved us
and sent his Son as a sacrifice to take away our sins.
1 JOHN 4:10

Have Faith in God

March 22

*D*o you know that it's possible to have faith in faith? We start believing that our faith is what saves us and our faith is what keeps us going. Wrong! Faith is what gets us to the One who saves us and keeps us going. What good is it just to have faith? Unless our faith points to the all-powerful, all-loving, totally just, completely holy God of the universe, it won't do us any good.

So you see, it isn't enough just to have faith.
JAMES 2:17

GET ON THE PLANE

March 23

*L*et's say you made a reservation to fly to Hawaii. When the day of your flight arrives, you drive to the airport. But rather than taking your seat on the plane, you watch the plane take off. Then you say, "See that plane? I have a reservation for that flight. My reservation is going to Hawaii." Your faith in God is like that reservation. Just as you fulfill your reservation by getting on the plane, you fulfill your faith in God by getting with His plan.

Faith that doesn't show itself by good deeds is no faith at all—it is dead and useless.
JAMES 2:17

_____

_____

_____

_____

_____

March 24

BE A GOOD DOER

*A*s Christians we have a responsibility to turn our thinking into action because doing so shows the world that our faith in God really matters. Our faith is the "assurance" of what we believe God is going to do in the future, and it is the "evidence" of what God wants to do through us here on earth (Hebrews 11:1). Others will see our faith in action before they see our faith in heaven.

"I can't see your faith if you don't have good deeds, but I will show you my faith through my good deeds."
JAMES 2:18

_____

_____

_____

_____

_____

In Search of Self-Worth

*O*ur society holds self-esteem in great esteem. But the Bible isn't as politically correct as our society would prefer. It lays the truth on the line: We are all sinners. We are fatally flawed. There is not one good thing about us. The Bible also tells us that we are loved by God. That's where we should find our sense of self-worth.

> *"For God so loved the world that he gave his only Son, so that everyone*
> *who believes in him will not perish but have eternal life."*
> JOHN 3:16

Prayer

March 26

*P*rayer is simply talking to God. When it's hard to get started, try beginning your prayers by thanking God for who He is and for the world He has created. You can say that you are sorry for the wrong things you have done. You can pray for others, too. And last, you shouldn't hesitate to ask for God's help with your problems. Prayer is your direct link to God, and He's listening.

> *"When you pray, go away by yourself, shut the door behind you, and pray to your Father secretly.*
> *Then your Father, who knows all secrets, will reward you. . .because your Father*
> *knows exactly what you need even before you ask him!"*
> MATTHEW 6:6, 8

THE SOUL OF STEWARDSHIP

There is a good barometer for measuring how you feel about God: money. Your attitude about money reveals much about your relationship with God. "Stewardship" is the way you handle what God has given you. Stewardship involves realizing that everything you have comes from God.

"Bring all the tithes into the storehouse so there will be enough food in my Temple.
If you do," says the LORD Almighty, "I will open the windows of heaven for you."
MALACHI 3:10

_____

_____

_____

_____

_____

COMMIT YOURSELF

We all make a hundred decisions a day, but our commitments are few and far between. At some point in your life, you probably made a decision to follow Christ. Great decision! But until you committed yourself to Christ, your decision probably didn't lead to any changes in your life. Deciding to follow Christ is acknowledging that He needs to take control of your life and change you from the inside out. Committing to Christ means you actually give Him that control.

"No one can become my disciple without giving up everything for me."
LUKE 14:33

_____

_____

_____

_____

_____

No Limits

*H*uman love is conditional. But God's love is unconditional. He loved us before we were even interested in Him. He continues to love us even as we disappoint Him with our immature attitudes. And His love for us prevails although our conduct may offend Him. There is nothing we could do that would make God love us less.

> *Whether we are high above the sky or in the deepest ocean, nothing*
> *in all creation will ever be able to separate us from the love of God*
> *that is revealed in Christ Jesus our Lord.*
> ROMANS 8:39

_____

_____

_____

_____

_____

God's Day

*I*n the Old Testament, the "Sabbath" referred to the seventh day of the week. Whether we observe the Sabbath on Saturday or Sunday, God wants us to set aside one day a week for Him by resting from our routine and work. Unfortunately, most of us are as busy on God's day as we are the rest of the week. May we suggest a new approach to His day? Set it apart for God. Celebrate His involvement in the big and small stuff in your life.

> *"Remember to observe the Sabbath day by keeping it holy."*
> EXODUS 20:8

_____

_____

_____

_____

_____

WORRIES

March 31

Consider the obstacles that Jesus faced in His life. He didn't worry about the course of events in His life. Jesus knew that His heavenly Father was in control. Worries can be a burdensome weight on your life if you carry them around with you. But it is foolish to do so (and utterly unnecessary). Instead of fretting, spend your mental energy trusting God to work things out. Jesus let His Father be in control, and so should you.

"I tell you, don't worry about everyday life—whether you have enough food, drink, and clothes."
MATTHEW 6:25

LAUGH IT UP

April 1

Nobody likes a sore loser, but more than that, nobody likes someone who can't laugh at himself. We're not talking about laughing at your own jokes (which is also annoying). Our advice is to lighten up and enjoy life. You might even ask God to put a little laughter on your lips and humor in your heart.

"He will yet fill your mouth with laughter and your lips with shouts of joy."
JOB 8:21

The Depths of Joy

*H*appiness is a hot commodity these days. If we feel good, we're happy. Simple as that. When people say, "I just want to be happy," they are really saying, "I just want to feel good all the time." Life isn't like that. That's why we need to seek joy rather than happiness. Happiness comes from the things of this world; joy comes from God.

Always be full of joy in the Lord. I say it again—rejoice!
PHILIPPIANS 4:4

_____

_____

_____

_____

_____

Divine Design

*T*eenagers quickly learn that it is easier to ask forgiveness than to ask permission. We often take the same approach with God. We make plans for what we want, and we leave God out of the planning process. Then we involve God by asking Him to "bless" what we have already decided to do. Don't treat God like a magic wand that you wave over your plans. Involve Him at the very beginning.

Trust in the LORD with all your heart; do not depend on your own understanding.
Seek his will in all you do, and he will direct your paths.
PROVERBS 3:5–6

_____

_____

_____

_____

_____

LITTLE THINGS HURT THE MOST

April 4

Not only do you please God when you control your anger, but you prevent the devil from using your anger to his advantage. It's the little things that do the most damage: sarcastic comments, cutting remarks, backbiting, undermining, and lying. This is the kind of anger that is most destructive, because it's out before you know it, or without your even noticing.

Don't let the sun go down while you are still angry, for anger gives a mighty foothold to the Devil.
EPHESIANS 4:26–27

April 5

THE POWER OF WORDS

More than any other force on earth, words can hurt, discourage, depress, and even destroy others. James understood that the tongue is capable of doing "enormous damage" (James 3:5). A careful tongue is a tongue in control, especially when it comes to the small stuff—those casual comments, those words spoken "under our breath" that so easily slip out and so quickly do damage.

We all make many mistakes, but those who control their tongues can also control themselves in every other way.
JAMES 3:2

YOUR FAMILY

*H*ospitality is often defined as the display of thoughtfulness to strangers and guests. We are often more kind to strangers and friends than we are to the members of our family. The "outsiders" get the best part of us, while the people in our own household get the worst. There's an old saying that goes, "Familiarity breeds contempt." Here's another old saying: "I command you to love each other" (John 15:17).

Dear friends, let us continue to love one another, for love comes from God.
I JOHN 4:7

_____

_____

_____

_____

_____

ARE YOU DEVOTED?

*I*t's easy to focus on your devotions rather than the object of your devotions. As you go through this book (or your own Bible study outline), do your best to focus on God rather than the discipline of daily devotions. Let's meet with Him daily to get to know Him better, to learn what pleases Him, and to find out what He wants us to do.

"Get to know the God of your ancestors. Worship and serve him with your whole heart and with a willing mind."
I CHRONICLES 28:9

_____

_____

_____

_____

_____

GOD'S WILL

April 8

*P*eople make God's will harder than it needs to be. Jesus simply summed up God's will for your life when He said, "You must love the Lord your God with all your heart, all your soul, all your mind, and all your strength. . .[and] love your neighbor as yourself" (Mark 12:30–31). That's it. Just stay focused on God.

God is working in you, giving you the desire to obey him and the power to do what pleases him.
PHILIPPIANS 2:13

April 9

PRAY EARNESTLY

*T*here's a reason God wants us to devote ourselves to prayer—it works. He's given us prayer so we can tell Him our deepest needs. Prayer is so much more than reciting words. It's talking with God about everything in your life, from the small stuff to your big concerns. And when you pray earnestly, God promises to answer in ways that will amaze you.

"I will answer them before they even call to me. While they are still talking
to me about their needs, I will go ahead and answer their prayers!"
ISAIAH 65:24

GENEROSITY

*M*ost people consider themselves to be generous. But true generosity requires more than plunking a few coins into the Salvation Army bucket at Christmas. How much you give away is irrelevant if your motive isn't right. Your giving should make a difference in the lives of people in need. Let God lead your decisions for where and how much to give.

Tell them to use their money to do good. They should be rich in good works and should give generously to those in need, always being ready to share with others whatever God has given them.
1 TIMOTHY 6:18

CIRCUMSTANCES

*M*uch of what happens in life, whether insignificant or catastrophic, is beyond your control. But you can choose how you will respond to these situations. Instead of being infuriated by your own inability to alter events, be thankful that God is all-powerful and has control over all things. He can change the circumstances or give you the strength to endure them.

I have learned the secret of living in every situation, whether it is with a full stomach or empty, with plenty or little. For I can do everything with the help of Christ who gives me the strength I need.
PHILIPPIANS 4:12–13

DEVELOPING THE RIGHT HABITS

April 12

*D*eveloping new habits doesn't come automatically. First, you must identify the conduct in your life that needs to stop. Next, you need to learn from God's Word the type of lifestyle God wants you to have. Then you need to implement the new pattern of living—repeating it constantly so that it becomes a habit.

We can tell who are children of God and who are children of the Devil. Anyone who does not obey God's commands and does not love other Christians does not belong to God.
1 JOHN 3:10

April 13

LOVING GOD

*T*he greatest emotion—and the only one God asks us to have in response to His love and grace—is love. Loving God, however, takes effort and sacrifice. It doesn't flow naturally. That's why God commands us to do it. This isn't emotional love but love that understands and truly wants the best for the other person. When you want the best for God, you give your best to God.

*"And you must love the L*ORD *your God with all your heart, all your soul, and all your strength."*
DEUTERONOMY 6:5

GLOWING IN THE NIGHT

April 14

A stealth Christian thinks nothing of adopting some of the "harmless" habits and ways of the world. There are two problems with this. First, "you can't ignore God and get away with it. You will always reap what you sow!" (Galatians 6:7). Second, God wants us to be "the light of the world—like a city on a mountain, glowing in the night for all to see" (Matthew 5:14).

> *"Don't hide your light under a basket! Instead, put it on a stand and let it shine for all."*
> MATTHEW 5:15

_____

_____

_____

_____

_____

THE WORTH OF THE WORD

April 15

T o be effective, your Bible must serve a greater purpose than as a decoration for your bookcase, a dust-collector on your nightstand, or a paperweight on your desk. It must be opened. It must be read. And it must be studied. Don't neglect the personal message that God has waiting for you in His Word. What He has to say to you will change your life (but only if you read it).

> *Your word is a lamp for my feet and a light for my path.*
> PSALM 119:105

_____

_____

_____

_____

_____

ANGELS ALL AROUND

*A*ngels are very real spirit beings created by God for a single purpose: to serve and worship God. Now, God has done an amazing thing by ordering His angels to protect us, but we should never put angels on a pedestal. What we should do is worship and thank God for sending His angels to help and protect us, even when we don't realize it.

> *He orders his angels to protect you wherever you go. They will hold*
> *you with their hands to keep you from striking your foot on a stone.*
> PSALM 91:11–12

April 17

RESPONDING TO GOD

*G*od gave us a free will, and we can decide for ourselves whether we will obey His commandments. You shouldn't have to pop a cranial corpuscle to decide whether you should follow God's plan for your life. He knows everything, He loves you, and He is wholly holy.

> *"Anyone who listens to my teaching and obeys me is wise, like a person who builds a house on solid rock.*
> *Though the rain comes in torrents and the floodwaters rise and the winds beat against that house,*
> *it won't collapse, because it is built on rock."*
> MATTHEW 7:24–25

Working Together

*A*n interesting thing happens when people in a group work against each other rather than with each other: nothing. All of the productivity is slowed when people are more concerned about their own interests than the goal of the group. Instead of worrying about your own interests, become aware of how the strengths of others in the group can complement your weaknesses. Each one of you plays a necessary part in accomplishing God's plan.

God has given each of us the ability to do certain things well.
ROMANS 12:6

_____

_____

_____

_____

_____

Overcoming Adversity

*G*od did not create evil or suffering. He created human beings who were perfect and free to choose or not to choose God. The bad news is that the perfect humans chose evil over God, thereby introducing sin and its consequences into the world (Romans 5:12). But all was not lost. God gave us the person of Jesus, who overcame evil and brought us God's forgiveness (Romans 5:15). He suffered on our behalf and knows what it's like for us to suffer.

Since he himself has gone through suffering and temptation, he is able to help us when we are being tempted.
HEBREWS 2:18

_____

_____

_____

_____

_____

THE FINAL CURTAIN?

April 20

*M*any people believe there's nothing after death, but the Bible teaches otherwise. The biggest authority in the world is Jesus. From the time John was beheaded to the time Jesus was put to death on the cross, Jesus knew death. Yet He also knew that He would ultimately defeat death, and not just for Himself, but for all who believe in Him.

> *"I am the resurrection and the life. Those who believe in me, even though they die like everyone else,*
> *will live again. They are given eternal life for believing in me and will never perish."*
> JOHN 11:25–26

April 21

GOD IS THINKING ABOUT YOU

*T*he Bible identifies God as our heavenly Father. He isn't a father who is too busy with His work that He doesn't have time for you. You are God's work. You are what He thinks about all day long. Since before the world was created, God knew and loved you. As you go about your hectic schedule today, take a little time to think about God—He is thinking about you.

> *How precious are your thoughts about me, O God! They are innumerable!*
> *I can't even count them; they outnumber the grains of sand!*
> PSALM 139:17–18

CONFUSE YOUR ENEMIES

*W*e have a tendency to love people who love us and to hate those who hate us. We want to get even, settle the score, and stand up for our rights when we've been wronged. Jesus calls us to an unusual response in which we show love and forgiveness toward our enemies. That type of response may change the heart of your enemy.

Instead, do what the Scriptures say: "If your enemies are hungry, feed them. If they are thirsty, give them something to drink, and they will be ashamed of what they have done to you."
ROMANS 12:20

_____

_____

_____

_____

_____

HOW TO BE SIGNIFICANT

April 23

*E*veryone wants his or her life to count for something, to be meaningful, and to make a difference. Real significance is not a matter of greatness or fame or influence. True significance is found in serving. Jesus was the most significant person the world has ever known, yet He acted like a servant. If you want your life to have significance and meaning, then look for ways that you can serve other people.

Then he said, "Anyone who wants to be the first must take last place and be the servant of everyone else."
MARK 9:35

_____

_____

_____

_____

_____

FORGIVENESS IS BIG

April 24

*F*orgiveness is very big in God's eyes. Without His forgiveness of our sins, we couldn't get near God because He wouldn't get near us. We should thank God every day for His forgiveness, which opens the door to our relationship with Him. But God asks more of us. He wants us to forgive others, especially those who have hurt us deeply. That's a very tough assignment. And yet that's exactly why God asks us to do it.

You must make allowance for each other's faults and forgive the person who offends you.
COLOSSIANS 3:13

April 25

FORGIVENESS IS NOT AN OPTION

*W*hy do we find it hard to forgive others? They have hurt us and consequently don't deserve our forgiveness. Besides, they haven't asked for our forgiveness. We need to remember that in our relationship to God, we are the offenders and God is the offended. We have hurt God and don't deserve His forgiveness, yet He didn't wait until we asked Him to forgive us. Out of His deep love for us, He forgave us while we were still in rebellion against Him.

Remember, the Lord forgave you, so you must forgive others.
COLOSSIANS 3:13

THE OTHER SIDE OF FORGIVENESS

*D*oes God really forgive us in the same way we forgive others? God has forgiven us, and He continues to forgive us. He doesn't "constantly accuse us" and "has removed our rebellious acts as far away from us as the east is from the west" (Psalm 103:9, 12). He doesn't keep any records. How unlike us! Yet that's what God wants us to be—unlike our sinful selves and more like Him.

> *"If you forgive those who sin against you, your heavenly Father will forgive you."*
> MATTHEW 6:14

_____

_____

_____

_____

_____

HOLINESS

*B*ecause Christ paid the penalty for your sins, God sees you as righteous. Your sins (past and future) are gone. This is positional holiness—how God sees you. While positional holiness happens immediately, practical holiness happens gradually as you align your thinking with God's precepts. As your thoughts change, your conduct will change. You'll find increasing evidence of holiness in your life as you remain diligent in your devotion to God.

> *You must be holy in everything you do, just as God—who chose you to be his children—is holy.*
> I PETER 1:15

_____

_____

_____

_____

_____

You Aren't Stuck with "Plan B"

April 28

*F*or many people, divorce has occurred in their lives. Are they stuck living in an inferior "Plan B" world because God doesn't like what they have done? God does not reserve His love for those who follow His intended "Plan A." We have a God who is in the business of restoring relationships. God may hate divorce (Malachi 2:16), but He is always ready to forgive and receive us back into fellowship with Him.

> *"Since they are no longer two but one, let no one separate them, for God has joined them together."*
> MATTHEW 19:6

April 29

Deceit

*W*hen you live a long time with deceit, it begins to take its toll on your body and your mind. You become frantic and depressed as you must constantly create more lies in order to cover what you have already said and done. On the other hand, when you confess the lies and begin to live in truth—when honesty becomes your policy—you will experience a joy and a level of freedom you never thought possible.

> *The LORD hates those who don't keep their word, but he delights in those who do.*
> PROVERBS 12:22

GOD WON'T TEMPT YOU

*T*here's a difference between trials and temptations. A trial is something that happens to us through outer circumstances or our own actions. God allows trials in our lives because they have the potential to make us "partners with Christ in his suffering" (1 Peter 4:13). On the other hand, a temptation can entice us to do the wrong thing. God is never tempted to do wrong. God doesn't tempt us to do wrong, either.

> *God is never tempted to do wrong, and he never tempts anyone else either.*
> JAMES 1:13

WHY NOT?

May 1

*H*ave you ever had a discussion with a child? Every statement you make is greeted with "Why?" You don't blame the child for asking, "Why?" But when an adult questions everything people tell him, it can be annoying. We all need to ask questions and get information, but when our questions keep us from getting things done, they stop being helpful. At some point you have to stop asking "Why?" and ask "Why not?"

> *"I know all the things you do, that you are neither hot nor cold. I wish you were one or the other!"*
> REVELATION 3:15

CHOICES, CHOICES

May 2

Choices. Some are insignificant. Others are monumental. Behavior is also a matter of choice. Every day we choose between following the desires of our sinful nature and following the direction of the Holy Spirit. When you are faced with the choice of following your sinful nature or following the Holy Spirit, remind yourself of the consequences of each choice.

Once we, too, were foolish and disobedient. . . . But then God our Savior showed us his kindness and love.
He saved us, not because of the good things we did, but because of his mercy.
TITUS 3:3–5

May 3

GOD ISN'T LIKE US

We make lousy judges. We make snap judgments based on what people look like, what they say, and what they do. No wonder we are so slow to forgive others. We can thank God that He isn't like us. God looks beyond appearance to the inner qualities—such as faith and character—that make us who we are. We can trust God to judge us fairly and honestly.

"The LORD doesn't make decisions the way you do! People judge by outward appearance."
1 SAMUEL 16:7

Develop the Inner You

*O*kay, so there's a downside to God's judgment. He sees the real us from the inside out; there's no fooling Him. Before we act, God knows what we're thinking. That could be more than a little unnerving, but He's not intruding into your private life. God simply knows you completely (and loves you anyway). Spend time developing the inner you. Pay attention to qualities like character and integrity. These are the things that count in God's all-seeing eyes.

> *"But the LORD looks at a person's thoughts and intentions."*
> I SAMUEL 16:7

God's Word Is Timeless

*T*he Bible doesn't have an expiration date. It is timeless. Its description of God is never obsolete because God's nature never changes. He is the same yesterday, today, and forever, so what was written about Him centuries ago by Moses and the apostle Paul is still true. God's plan to connect with the human race through Jesus Christ hasn't changed. The truth of the Bible will never be outdated.

> *Your justice is eternal, and your law is perfectly true. As pressure and stress bear down on me, I find joy in your commands.*
> PSALM 119:142–143

HOW MUCH IS ENOUGH?

May 6

*H*ow much is enough? Jesus wasn't too concerned about possessions. He was born in a borrowed stable and was buried in a borrowed tomb. Don't think that Jesus was setting a pattern that requires you to rent your furniture. The relevant issue is whether you are depending on your possessions for your security or your happiness.

> *"Real life is not measured by how much we own. . . . Yes, a person is a fool*
> *to store up earthly wealth but not have a rich relationship with God."*
> LUKE 12:15, 21

May 7

POWER UP

*T*he way people normally acquire power is on the outside. They work out with a bunch of weights, they go to college for a long time, or they work their way to the top of a company. God doesn't need these outward devices to give you power, and He doesn't need a lot of time. When you enter into a personal relationship with God through Christ, something amazing happens: You receive the power of the Holy Spirit, and it happens from the inside.

> *"When the Holy Spirit has come upon you, you will receive power."*
> ACTS 1:8

Sit Still

*H*ave you ever sat behind a young child in church? After the child has sat still for a few minutes, the fidgeting begins. That squirming child can be a metaphor for our lives with God. We are usually so busy fidgeting with the activities of life that we miss hearing what God wants to tell us. Stop fidgeting for a few moments each day. Read the Bible, and listen to what God is saying to you.

> *The LORD is wonderfully good to those who wait for him and seek him.*
> LAMENTATIONS 3:25

Judge Fairly

*G*od knows we can't help judging others, so He has intensified His request by reminding us that we will be judged according to how we judge others. In this matter of judging and being judged, what God is asking us to do is put ourselves in the other person's shoes. Just as we don't want to be judged unfairly, we shouldn't judge others unfairly. And if we do, we can expect unfair judgment to come our way.

> *"Stop judging others, and you will not be judged. For others will treat you as you treat them."*
> MATTHEW 7:1–2

WISDOM

May 10

There are two kinds of wisdom: worldly wisdom and spiritual wisdom. Worldly wisdom involves applying knowledge and human understanding to certain factual situations. Spiritual wisdom doesn't rely on human understanding. In fact, spiritual wisdom refers to a belief system that can be comprehended only through spiritual insight. Spiritual wisdom comes through the Holy Spirit and gives you insight into God's nature.

The wisdom we speak of is the secret wisdom of God. . . .
But we know these things because God has revealed them to us by his Spirit.
1 CORINTHIANS 2:7, 10

May 11

THE FRIENDSHIP FACTOR

Everyone wants to enjoy the loyalty, support, and companionship of a friend. You are there for your friends, and they are there for you. Jesus defined true friendship when He said, "Love each other in the same way that I love you" (John 15:12). You may never be asked to die for a friend, but there are many other ways you can make personal sacrifices for the benefit of your friends through your time, energy, and resources.

"I command you to love each other in the same way that I love you."
JOHN 15:12

How to Pray

Prayer involves more than just kneeling at a bedside with hands folded and eyes closed. Prayer involves effort. Sincere prayer requires a willingness to put some action behind what you are asking from God. After you pray for your family and neighbors, do something tangible to show your love for them. After you pray for world peace, show kindness to someone. Saying "Amen" doesn't end your prayer. It's the signal for your action to begin.

The earnest prayer of a righteous person has great power and wonderful results.
JAMES 5:16

_____

_____

_____

_____

What Makes a Good Sermon?

How does God talk to you? Don't forget that God also speaks to you through the sermons you hear. Most of us make the mistake of sitting in church as though we are members of an audience. That is the wrong approach. When we worship at church, God is the audience—we are the participants. True worship includes responding to the message that is preached—not just listening but actually applying what we have heard to our lives.

Then [Jesus] said, "Anyone who is willing to hear should listen and understand!"
MARK 4:8—9

_____

_____

_____

_____

THE BEST KIND OF HUMOR

May 14

The Bible doesn't say a lot about humor, but there are plenty of principles regarding joy. Humor for humor's sake is often pointless and sometimes demeaning. When humor brings joy to others, it serves a worthwhile purpose. You give people something rather than taking something away. When you use humor to bring joy to others, you help relieve them of sorrow (Jeremiah 31:13) and refresh them (Philemon 7). Most of all, you connect them with God (Psalm 16:11).

We were filled with laughter, and we sang for joy.
PSALM 126:2

_____

_____

_____

_____

May 15

WHERE IS YOUR AFFECTION?

Have you noticed the destructive power of greed? Even though we are aware of its potential dangers, the allure remains. Remember that money is neither good nor bad. It is the love of money that presents the problems. Money can never get you closer to God, but your attraction to it can keep you away from Him. Make sure your affections are for your Maker, not for your money.

People who long to be rich fall into temptation and are trapped by many
foolish and harmful desires that plunge them into ruin and destruction.
1 TIMOTHY 6:9

_____

_____

_____

_____

Begin Your Day with God

*K*ing David was a morning person. He loved to get up early and meet the Lord in prayer and meditation. You may not be the king of a country, but your calendar is no less busy than that of a full-time monarch. You have appointments to keep, decrees to declare, and duties to perform. It's not that God isn't available later in the day. You're the one who gets too busy for God.

> *Listen to my voice in the morning, LORD. Each morning I bring my requests to you and wait expectantly.*
> PSALM 5:3

_____

_____

_____

_____

_____

Remember Yesterday

*A*nother reason for beginning your day with God is that you can remember what God did for you yesterday. If you want to reflect on the stuff God has accomplished in your life, sit quietly in the early morning with your Bible and just reflect. Close your eyes and let Him bring to mind the wonderful things He did for you yesterday.

> *Understand, therefore, that the LORD your God is indeed God. He is the faithful God who keeps his covenant for a thousand generations and constantly loves those who love him and obey his commands.*
> DEUTERONOMY 7:9

_____

_____

_____

_____

_____

Boost Your Memory

May 18

*I*n the Old Testament, the great leader Joshua made it a practice to stack up twelve large stones (one for each of the tribes of Israel) whenever God did something for them. We're not suggesting that you make a rock pile in your front yard to mark a special time when God helped you, but a special calendar or journal in which you keep track of God's unusual provisions might work. Whatever you do, make an effort to remember.

I recall all you have done, O LORD; I remember your wonderful deeds of long ago.
PSALM 77:11

May 19

Leadership

*W*hen you are in charge, do you try to intimidate others and order people around? Modern leadership theory subscribes to the concept of "servant leadership." This was hailed as a groundbreaking management concept in the 1970s. Wow! It took society only a little more than nineteen centuries to catch on to what Jesus taught. If you want to be an effective leader, be a servant.

"But among you, those who are the greatest should take the lowest rank, and the leader should be like a servant."
LUKE 22:26

There's Time to Change

*Y*ou are never too old to start a personal relationship with God. And once you have connected with Him, it is never too late to have your life changed by Him. Now that we think about it, there does come a time when it is too late to respond to God. Death is the ultimate "too late" stage.

I am sure that God, who began the good work within you, will continue his work until it is finally finished on that day when Christ Jesus comes back again.
PHILIPPIANS 1:6

_____

_____

_____

_____

_____

Persecution

*P*ersecution for your faith can take different forms, and it usually involves suffering to one degree or another. Even verbal ridicule can be tough to take. If you suffer for being a Christian, no matter what the extent, you can rejoice in the fact that it's a privilege. Rejoice, because when you suffer for claiming the name of Christ, you are being identified with God.

It is no shame to suffer for being a Christian. Praise God for the privilege of being called by his wonderful name!
1 PETER 4:16

_____

_____

_____

_____

_____

FAITH ABIDES

May 22

*E*very single day of their lives, people have faith in stuff. They trust the weather forecaster who says it's not going to rain. They drive on the freeway and have faith that none of the other drivers are going to hit them head-on. You need faith to live, or else you'd sit at home in the dark and do nothing. Believing in God is not for the simple or the weak. It's for thoughtful people who know that without faith, you can't ultimately experience and know God.

"A righteous person will live by faith."
HEBREWS 10:38

May 23

LET GOD HAVE A TURN TO TALK

*W*hat is your definition of prayer? The correct answer is "talking with God." Conversation, by its definition, requires two-way communication. Maybe you're thinking that prayers have to be one-way only (you to God) because God never replies. Well, He does. You'll have to stop talking and listen.

"The Maker of the heavens and earth—the LORD is his name—says this:
Ask me and I will tell you some remarkable secrets about what is going to happen here."
JEREMIAH 33:2–3

DELIGHT IN SEEKING GOD

*O*ne of the greatest pleasures in life is seeking God. When we seek God at any level—whether skeptically or wholeheartedly—we eventually discover someone who wants to give us abundant life (John 10:10). Don't make the mistake of seeking God for temporary solutions to your problems. He can do anything, but He delights in giving you long-lasting peace of mind and heart, and joy unlike anything you can experience on your own.

> *"If you look for me in earnest, you will find me when you seek me."*
> JEREMIAH 29:13

SUCCESS

*F*rom a spiritual viewpoint, success is determined by the ultimate destiny of your soul. If you really want to have success that matters and will last forever, you must be willing to abandon the things of the world and invest your energies in spiritual matters.

> *"If any of you wants to be my follower, you must put aside your selfish ambition, shoulder your cross, and follow me. If you try to keep your life for yourself, you will lose it. But if you give up your life for me, you will find true life."*
> MATTHEW 16:24–25

BE A GOD PLEASER

May 26

God enjoys our efforts to please Him. Because He's God and He already loves us as much as He can, you can't say that God loves us any more or feels better about us when we please Him. But He does respond when we do the things that please Him. Of course the one who is happiest is the one who does the things that please God.

Try to find out what is pleasing to the Lord.
EPHESIANS 5:10

May 27

THE BEAUTY OF CREATION

Our world is filled with beauty, but often we are too busy to notice. Imagine that you attended an art exhibition featuring brilliant paintings by a local artist. If you blasted through the gallery without looking at the paintings, you would insult the artist. You would also be depriving yourself of the beauty on display. So it is with the world around you. God is the Master Artist who creatively designed the beauty in nature. Don't rush through His gallery.

The heavens tell of the glory of God. The skies display his marvelous craftsmanship.
PSALM 19:1

More Than Mere Interest

*T*here's a difference between merely being interested in God and truly believing in Him. A lot of people have a curiosity about God, but they say they won't believe in Him until they have proof of His existence. The world has all the information about God that is required for belief. The Bible gives the historical facts, and Christians are the living proof. Seeing is not required for believing, because there is sufficient evidence for anyone who is sincerely seeking to find God.

"Blessed are those who haven't seen me and believe anyway."
JOHN 20:29

Be a Servant

*G*od's kingdom is unlike man's kingdoms and governments. Christianity is based on service to others, so Christian leaders must be interested in serving rather than being served. Our example is Jesus Christ. He did not come to earth to be served by others but to serve. You may never be asked to give your life for someone else, but that attitude of self-sacrificing service should be the mark of your Christianity.

"But among you it should be quite different. Whoever wants to be a leader among you must be your servant."
MATTHEW 20:26

Worth the Effort

May 30

*W*hen an athlete steps up on the award platform, there is no regret about time spent in training. Just like an athlete who adheres to a strict fitness and diet program, a Christian must stay away from things that would be detrimental to living a life that honors God. The training program for Christianity (prayer, Bible reading, fellowship with Christians) can bring you closer to God on a daily basis, and that prize makes the self-discipline worthwhile.

Remember that in a race everyone runs, but only one person gets the prize.
You also must run in such a way that you will win.
1 Corinthians 9:24

May 31

A Mother's Love

*I*t takes so little to make your mother happy. She loves you for who you are. You are the fruit of her womb, the apple of her eye, the crown of her head. "Such a good boy," she'll tell you as she cups your face in her hands. "Such a sweet girl," she'll say as she embraces you. All she needs from you is a note or a call telling her that you love her and that you wouldn't be where you are without her.

May she who gave you birth be happy.
Proverbs 23:25

WORDS OF THE HEART

*W*e often put on a facade of being spiritual, but it is just a show. If we do this long and often, we begin to fool ourselves into thinking we are spiritual when we really aren't. How can you tell what's really in your heart? Listen to the words that come out of your mouth. If you hear lying, gossip, criticism, or bitterness, then you have a serious heart problem. But if you're speaking words of truth, kindness, and encouragement, then your heart is in great spiritual shape.

"Whatever is in your heart determines what you say."
LUKE 6:45

THE PEACE OF GOD

*T*he peace of God is a gift, because there's no way we can generate it on our own. The peace of God permeates every part of our being. When we give God our burdens, He removes our anxiety. When we give God our doubts and fears, He replaces them with confidence. When we trust God, obey God, and depend on God in all circumstances, He gives us His gift of peace.

If you do this, you will experience God's peace, which is far more wonderful than the human mind can understand.
PHILIPPIANS 4:7

PRACTICAL PEACE

June 3

The opposite of peace is war, and that's exactly what happens in our lives when God's peace is missing. It's a war within us, caused by sin, fear, doubt, and anxiety. We lump everything together and call it stress, but it's a little more complicated than that. None of this is a secret to God. He's completely aware of all the details. He's just waiting for us to ask Him to handle them for us. He won't intrude; we must invite Him. When we do, He'll come to our rescue.

His peace will guard your hearts and minds as you live in Christ Jesus.
PHILIPPIANS 4:7

June 4

PEACE WITH GOD

The Bible says that we are God's enemies because we are sinners (Romans 5:10). The only way to end the war with God is to raise the white flag of surrender. We have to accept God's terms for peace, which center on the person and work of Jesus. When we do that, we experience the ultimate peace—peace with God.

Therefore, since we have been made right in God's sight by faith, we have peace with God because of what Jesus Christ our Lord has done for us.
ROMANS 5:1

Marriage

*M*arriage is in God's plan for some, but it may not be His plan for others. If you are married, then God wants you wholeheartedly devoted to your spouse in love, loyalty, and respect. If you are single, your life should be marked by sexual and moral purity.

> *As the Scriptures say, "A man leaves his father and mother and is joined to his wife, and the two are united into one." This is a great mystery, but it is an illustration of the way Christ and the church are one.*
> EPHESIANS 5:31–32

Prayer Works

*D*on't evaluate the effectiveness of your prayers solely on the basis of whether God gives you what you asked for. Sometimes He may respond in the way you asked; other times He may deny your request because it is not in your best interests; or He may postpone action for reasons that are unknown to you. Prayer is not designed to give you everything. The purpose of prayer is to connect you with God.

> *Don't worry about anything; instead, pray about everything. Tell God what you need, and thank him for all he has done.*
> PHILIPPIANS 4:6

Thinking and Doing

*F*ollowing God requires thinking and doing. You have to know what is right, and you must put that knowledge into action. It takes both knowledge and action to pursue God's principles. God equips you in both of these areas. He has given us His Word—the Bible—so we know what is right and wrong. And He has given us the Holy Spirit to empower our actions.

Solid food is for those who are mature, who have trained themselves to recognize the difference between right and wrong and then do what is right.
2 HEBREWS 5:14

The God Who Is

A lot of people think God is Santa Claus. They see God as a powerful deity, and their relationship is based on what they hope He will do for them. People with this view of God have little idea of who God really is—the God who loves them and who wants very much to have a personal relationship with them. The only way to change this view is to seek God for who He is.

He prayed, "O Lord, God of Israel, there is no God like you in all of heaven and earth."
2 CHRONICLES 6:14

With God's Help

*P*eople ask God for help all the time, don't they? Not really. They ask for physical stuff, they ask for good health, and they ask for help when they're in trouble, but they don't ask for help where they really need it—in their spiritual lives. That's where we all need God, who is the only One who can help us spiritually. God helps us because it's in His nature to help.

"You keep your promises and show unfailing love to all who obey you and are eager to do your will."
2 CHRONICLES 6:14

_____

_____

_____

_____

_____

Connecting with God

*D*o you ever feel as if you're not good enough to please God? That's understandable, because you aren't. But Jesus is, and He can be our connection to God. Celebrate the fact that despite your faults, you can belong to God because Christ provides the perfection that you need.

"Unless you believe that I am who I say I am, you will die in your sins. . . . And the one who sent me is with me— he has not deserted me. For I always do those things that are pleasing to him."
JOHN 8:24, 29

_____

_____

_____

_____

_____

DON'T PUT GOD IN A BOX

*D*oes your life have meaning and purpose? If it doesn't, then perhaps you've put God in a box. You keep Him around for those times when you need Him to help you. But when things are going well, you keep Him in your little box and get along quite well all by yourself. He wants to do more than solve your problems. God wants to give you direction and purpose every day of your life.

*For who is God except the L*ORD*? Who but our God is a solid rock?*
PSALM 18:31

_____

_____

_____

_____

_____

NATURE'S THEOLOGY

*Y*ou don't have to attend seminary to gain insights into God's character. You need only to walk outdoors and look up—or look down. Nature reveals the enormity and power of God. It also reveals His creativity and attention to detail. Learn about God as you observe Him in nature.

From the time the world was created, people have seen the earth and sky
and all that God made.
ROMANS 1:20

_____

_____

_____

_____

_____

SETTLE FOR THE BEST

There will come a day when you realize that God wants more for you than you could possibly want for yourself. As you read His Word and talk with Him through prayer, you are going to gain a greater appreciation for who God is and what His will is for you. He wants you to live your life fully while you anticipate the amazing life waiting for you in heaven.

"For I know the plans I have for you," says the LORD.
"They are plans for good and not for disaster, to give you a future and a hope."
JEREMIAH 29:11

WANTING WHAT GOD
HASN'T GIVEN YOU

Envy begins when we see someone else who has what we want, and our desire is to have it for ourselves. If there is something you desire but God hasn't given it to you, He has a reason. Don't be envious of anything that God doesn't want you to have.

You are jealous for what others have, and you can't possess it, so you fight and quarrel to take it away
from them. And yet the reason you don't have what you want is that you don't ask God for it.
JAMES 4:2

TRUST IN GOD

*W*henever we believe God is going to do something because we need it right now, we put our faith in the wrong place. What if He doesn't? Is your faith inadequate, or does God have something else to teach you? When your faith demands miracles, you think that if you believe hard enough, God will do something. It is much more effective to put your complete trust in God rather than in what you need from God.

"I do believe, but help me not to doubt!"
MARK 9:24

_____

_____

_____

_____

_____

PROMISES

*A*ren't you glad that God keeps His promises? He is totally reliable. And because He is, we can relax in our relationship with Him. Other people need to have the same sense of certainty in their relationships with you. They need to know that you are reliable and that you keep your promises. Promise less than you expect to do so that you can deliver more than you promised.

By that same mighty power, he has given us all of his rich
and wonderful promises.
2 PETER 1:4

_____

_____

_____

_____

_____

THE MOST IMPORTANT APPOINTMENT

*D*oes it seem like a good idea to put God at the top of your appointment list? Of course it does. He's the most important person in the world to you, and His plans for you are the most important tasks. Seek God and what He wants for you every day; and to help you remember, put His name in your appointment book. That's one daily meeting you don't want to miss.

In the morning you will see the glorious presence of the Lord.
EXODUS 16:7

_____

_____

_____

_____

_____

PRIORITIES

*H*as anyone ever told you to "arrange your priorities"? They're asking you to put goals and events in order of importance. God has deliberately called you out of the ordinary activities to a higher level of living. He wants you to structure your life in a way that makes Him your highest priority. Then everything else will fall into its proper place.

No, O people, the Lord has already told you what is good,
and this is what he requires: to do what is right, to love mercy,
and to walk humbly with your God.
MICAH 6:8

_____

_____

_____

_____

Avoiding Temptation

June 19

*W*e all struggle with temptation. It's not always a matter of weakness. Sometimes it is just a matter of plain stupidity. We stupidly put ourselves in the path of temptation when we could have avoided it altogether. Start being smart about resisting temptation. Decide ahead of time what you won't do, where you won't go, and what you won't watch. It's just a lot easier to stay away from temptation to begin with.

> *Humble yourselves before God. Resist the Devil, and he will flee from you.*
> JAMES 4:7

_____

_____

_____

_____

_____

June 20

Use Your Burdens

*W*hen you ask God to take away your burdens, you deny yourself the opportunity to grow in your faith. We don't believe in God because life is easy and we have everything we need. We come to God because we recognize our desperate situation. And once we align ourselves with God personally through Christ, our faith grows because we are aware we need Christ in us to live each day.

> *You can be sure that the more we suffer for Christ, the more God will shower us with his comfort through Christ.*
> 2 CORINTHIANS 1:5

_____

_____

_____

_____

_____

GOALS

The best goal you could ever have is to know God better. All of your energy should be focused on being like Christ in your actions and your thoughts. Everything else will seem insignificant compared to the indescribable wonder of knowing God and realizing His love for you.

I am focusing all my energies on this one thing: Forgetting the past and looking forward to what lies ahead,
I strain to reach the end of the race and receive the prize for which God, through Christ Jesus, is calling us up to heaven.
PHILIPPIANS 3:13–14

_____

_____

_____

_____

_____

DISCIPLINE

Following God requires that you stay in spiritual shape. Spiritual training requires a daily regimen of studying God's Word and spending quality time with Him in prayer. Exercising only once a week won't keep you physically fit. And you can't really know God by going to church only once a week. If you are serious about knowing God and following Him, you'll be serious about your spiritual fitness program.

All athletes practice strict self-control. They do it to win a prize
that will fade away, but we do it for an eternal prize.
1 CORINTHIANS 9:25

_____

_____

_____

_____

_____

REAL LIFE

June 23

*M*any people are fascinated with the possibility of the spiritual realm. A spiritual dimension could give more meaning to earthly existence and could have implications for life after death. That's what a religious leader named Nicodemus wanted to know. He asked Jesus how someone in the natural world could enter the spiritual realm. It takes a spiritual rebirth that happens through a belief in, and a relationship with, Jesus Himself.

"Humans can reproduce only human life,
but the Holy Spirit gives new life from heaven."
JOHN 3:6

June 24

PURPOSE

*D*o you ever wonder about your purpose in life? That is a fairly deep philosophical question, but the answer isn't too complicated. True purpose can be found only in matters that have eternal significance. A part of God's purpose for your life is to tell people about Him. Only God, through Christ, can change a life for eternity, and He has called you to deliver that message. He has called you for that purpose.

"Go into all the world and preach the Good News to everyone, everywhere."
MARK 16:15

Turn On the Ignition

June 25

*P*rayer is a powerful tool because it activates the power of God in your life. But He won't unleash His power unless you ask Him to, and the way you ask is through prayer. God is the engine that powers you, and the Holy Spirit is the fuel. Prayer is like the spark that ignites the Holy Spirit to drive God's power.

Let us come boldly to the throne of our gracious God. There we will receive his mercy,
and we will find grace to help us when we need it.
HEBREWS 4:16

Challenges

June 26

*T*he Bible says that you can expect tough times. But God equips you to handle anything that He allows to come your way. You shouldn't shy away from changes and challenges when you know that God is on your side. You should look forward to them. As God allows challenges into your life, don't worry about being pushed out of your comfort zone.

Those who wait on the LORD *will find new strength.*
They will fly high on wings like eagles. They will run and not grow weary. They will walk and not faint.
ISAIAH 40:31

THE KEY TO KNOWING YOURSELF

June 27

*W*e would suggest that you spend more time focused on God than on yourself. Studying Him and learning about Him take a lifetime, and even then you barely scratch the surface. Besides, getting to know God better inevitably leads to knowing yourself better. God created you in His own image. As you get closer to God, you will get closer to the real you.

We ask God to give you a complete understanding of what he wants to do in your lives,
and we ask him to make you wise with spiritual wisdom.
COLOSSIANS 1:9

_____

_____

_____

_____

_____

June 28

DEATH

*G*od has placed within each of us an eternal soul. From the moment of your conception, your soul exists forever. Your physical death is merely the cessation of your biological being, but your soul lives on. For those who know and love God, death is the beginning of the best part of their lives.

"Death is swallowed up in victory. O death, where is your victory?
O death, where is your sting?"
I CORINTHIANS 15:54–55

_____

_____

_____

_____

_____

LIKE A MIRROR

*E*very person is born with God's imprint, but every person is also born with sin's imprint. Those two imprints aren't equal, but sin obstructs our view of God and our longing for Him. God is much more powerful than our sins, but He won't take them away until we ask Him to. As God builds His character into ours, we become like mirrors reflecting His imprint and His glory, which others can clearly see.

As the Spirit of the Lord works within us, we become more and more like him and reflect his glory even more.
2 CORINTHIANS 3:18

RESPECT

*D*o you respect God? After all, He is the all-powerful, all-knowing, all-loving God who is intimately involved in the universe and in your life. You flagrantly disrespect Him when you are too busy to include Him in your life. You dishonor Him when you pursue your own petty desires instead of His plan. Everyone deserves your respect, and it will be easier to give it to them if you start by respecting God.

Show respect for everyone. Love your Christian brothers and sisters.
Fear God. Show respect for the king.
1 PETER 2:17

ADMIT YOUR MISTAKES

July 1

*A*dmitting a mistake is difficult for anyone, but there are some important reasons why you should. If you are making spiritual mistakes, then your relationship with God will be interrupted as long as you refuse to admit to God that you have done wrong. Don't hesitate to talk to God about your mistakes. After all, He noticed when you made them.

But no, you won't listen. So you are storing up terrible punishment for yourself because of your stubbornness in refusing to turn from your sin.
ROMANS 2:5

July 2

KEEP THE TRUTH TOGETHER

*T*elling the truth has become a lost art. We give out just enough information to keep us out of trouble, but not enough to honor God. He wants us to deal in whole truth. That's what it means to have integrity: to be "whole." If you want to be a person of integrity, don't break the truth into pieces. Keep it together, even if it invites criticism.

People with integrity have firm footing, but those who follow crooked paths will slip and fall.
PROVERBS 10:9

CRISIS

*Y*ou want a tranquil life, but at some unexpected time, you'll be hit by a crisis. Consider that your crisis can be an opportunity to grow closer to God. When the money runs out, or your health is in jeopardy, or the children are in trouble, you can turn to God and He will be there. It won't remain a crisis if God is in charge.

> *Those who plant in tears will harvest with shouts of joy. They weep as they go to plant their seed,*
> *but they sing as they return with the harvest.*
> PSALM 126:5–6

_____

_____

_____

_____

_____

DECLARE YOUR DEPENDENCE

*H*umankind declared its independence from God in the Garden of Eden when Adam and Eve believed the lie that they could live independently of God. Since then, we humans have been constantly struggling to do it our way. God knows that true independence is impossible. Jesus is the "true vine" (John 15:1), and unless we are connected to Him, we will never truly be productive.

> *"Remain in me, and I will remain in you. For a branch cannot produce fruit if*
> *it is severed from the vine, and you cannot be fruitful apart from me."*
> JOHN 15:4

_____

_____

_____

_____

_____

WORK ON YOUR CHARACTER

July 5

*Y*our character takes a long time to develop—a lifetime, in fact. It's a work that's always in progress, and it is built in small increments. It's more important to work on your character than your reputation, because your reputation can change. Your reputation will return—stronger than ever—as long as your character is rooted in God and not in your own strength.

"Unless you are faithful in small matters, you won't be faithful in large ones.
If you cheat even a little, you won't be honest with greater responsibilities."
LUKE 16:10

DESTINATION

July 6

A lot of people are very hostile toward anyone who tries to bring a godly influence into society. When you've been emotionally abused for your faith, just remember that this life is not your final destination. It's only transitory. You can look forward to time everlasting with God Himself. The best is yet to come.

"God blesses you when you are mocked and persecuted and lied about
because you are my followers. Be happy about it! Be very glad!
For a great reward awaits you in heaven."
MATTHEW 5:11–12

Cause and Effect

*I*f you do whatever you want for your own purposes without regard to God, then the consequences of your behavior will lead to your eternal separation from God. However, the consequences of your actions "will reap a harvest of blessing at the appropriate time" (Galatians 6:9) if your life pleases God.

> *You will always reap what you sow! Those who live only to satisfy their own sinful desires will harvest the consequences of decay and death. But those who live to please the Spirit will harvest everlasting life from the Spirit.*
> GALATIANS 6:7–8

_____

_____

_____

_____

_____

Spiritual Ambition

July 8

*I*t's only natural to have ambitions and to do everything necessary to attain your goals. But should you be ambitious just because it comes naturally? Jesus taught that gaining everything on earth—all the things that are supposed to make you happy—will still leave you emotionally bankrupt if you don't have a spiritual relationship with God. God wants you to live with ambition and purpose, but He doesn't want your focus to be self-centered.

> *"How do you benefit if you gain the whole world but lose or forfeit your own soul in the process?"*
> LUKE 9:25

_____

_____

_____

_____

_____

HAVE PATIENCE

July 9

*I*t's impossible to have patience unless you first have to wait. It's the waiting, which for most of us is difficult and unpleasant, that brings about the virtue of patience. It's an honorable thing to look for ways to wait so you can develop your patience. And what is the highest form of patience? Waiting on the Lord. That's where your patience is at its highest point.

If we look forward to something we don't have yet,
we must wait patiently and confidently.
ROMANS 8:25

_____

_____

_____

_____

_____

July 10

THE BEAUTY OF HONESTY

*H*onesty is like the glue that holds relationships together. However, dishonesty and deceit can tear the relationship apart. When you are tempted to violate the truth, ignore the excuses and look at your motives. Why would you want to jeopardize the relationship with the virus of dishonesty? Is it to protect you? Although the truth doesn't always come easily, God will honor you if you live honestly before Him.

It is an honor to receive an honest reply.
PROVERBS 24:26

_____

_____

_____

_____

_____

BABY TALK

Some Christians live out their spiritual lives like babies. Instead of growing up into full-size spiritual adults, they remain babies. Every one of us starts out as a baby in the Lord, but God doesn't want any of us to stay that way. His desire is that we grow into spiritually mature believers whose lives glorify Him.

> *You have been Christians a long time now, and you ought to be teaching others. Instead, you need someone to teach you again the basic things. . . . You are like babies who drink only milk and cannot eat solid food.*
> HEBREWS 5:12

DON'T BE A BABY

There are Christians who have no more spiritual maturity and discernment now than the day they were born again in Christ. How does this happen? The main reason is that they never get beyond baby food. Eventually we need to move beyond the basics to the deeper truths of God. This takes consistent study, prayer, and fellowship with other mature believers. Without these things, we remain babies.

> *A person who is living on milk isn't very far along in the Christian life and doesn't know much about doing what is right.*
> HEBREWS 5:13

WHAT YOU HAVE TO GIVE

July 13

*T*here is an art to gift giving. You have to know what the recipient needs. You want to choose a gift that will be appreciated and have some long-lasting value. These guidelines are useful for the usual gift-giving occasions, but they are also relevant in a spiritual context. There is a gift of a spiritual nature that you can give to your family and friends. It is a consistent testimony of a life committed wholeheartedly to God.

You have heard my vows, O God. You have given me an inheritance reserved for those who fear your name.
PSALM 61:5

_____

_____

_____

_____

_____

July 14

LEARN FROM A PET?

*O*ur pets can teach us a lot. It isn't too much of a stretch to compare the way we provide for our pets to the way God provides for us. That doesn't mean we are God's little pets. The comparison with pets has more to do with care and feeding. Just as our pets are totally dependent on us for their existence, we are completely dependent on God for all that we are and all that we have.

The godly are concerned for the welfare of their animals.
PROVERBS 12:10

_____

_____

_____

_____

_____

NOTORIETY

*Y*our desire to be well liked can be at odds with your faith in God. Claiming the name of Christ may alienate you from some groups. Jesus isn't very politically correct in most of society. Don't let your desire to be well liked impede your faith. The admiration of your friends is fickle, but God's love for you is forever.

> *"How do you benefit if you gain the whole world but lose your own soul in the process?*
> *Is anything worth more than your soul?"*
> MATTHEW 16:26

FULLY EQUIPPED

*T*here's nothing we can do to earn our salvation (Ephesians 2:8). The only work is the work of Christ on our behalf. Don't worry. God doesn't leave you on your own. God has given us His Word so we can grow into mature adult believers. As we read and study the Bible for ourselves, God will teach us through the Holy Spirit. If we make the effort to grow, God will fully equip us.

> *It is God's way of preparing us in every way, fully equipped*
> *for every good thing God wants us to do.*
> 2 TIMOTHY 3:17

STEWARDSHIP

July 17

*A*lthough God is not dependent on you for financial support, He is interested in how you spend your money. In fact, He wants you to use it to help others. He wants you to be generous, helping people in need and helping support the ministry of your church. God wants your financial giving to be a natural expression of your love for Him and for others.

If you are really eager to give, it isn't important how much you are able to give.
God wants you to give what you have, not what you don't have.
2 CORINTHIANS 8:12

July 18

IT'S NOT ENOUGH TO BELIEVE

*H*ow often have you heard someone say, "Oh, there are many ways to God. All that matters is that you believe." Do you believe that? Then all you are doing is believing in God, and your belief won't count for anything. On the other hand, when you believe that Jesus is God's only plan for your salvation, your belief will count for eternity.

Do you still think it's enough just to believe that there is one God?
Well, even the demons believe this, and they tremble in terror!
JAMES 2:19

REBELLION

*Y*ou probably don't consider yourself to be a rebellious person. It depends entirely on your mind-set. God designed you to be an individual with your own personality and style, but your actions and attitudes need to be within His plan for your life. When you intentionally leave God out of the details of your life, you are being defiant and rebelling against His authority.

> *"Yet I want your will, not mine."*
> MATTHEW 26:39

YOUR CIRCUMSTANCES AND GOD

*T*he story of Joseph is one of the most famous stories in the Bible. While it seemed that Joseph wasn't in control of his destiny, there was no question that God was with him every step of the way, directing his path, even when the days were dark. When it seems as though circumstances are outside your control and the world is against you, remain faithful to God. God promises to restore you for your own good and His glory.

> *"As far as I am concerned, God turned into good what you meant for evil."*
> GENESIS 50:20

BE PASSIONATE ABOUT IT

July 21

*Y*ou have to find your passion, define it, and then live it. After you discover what you are passionate about, you'll still have to do other things. The trick is to maintain your focus. God has created you, knows your innermost thoughts, and has a purpose for your life. Ask Him to reveal it to you, and then pursue it passionately.

> *But [Jesus] replied, "I must preach the Good News of the Kingdom of God*
> *in other places, too, because that is why I was sent."*
> LUKE 4:43

_____

_____

_____

_____

_____

July 22

GET IN THE GAME

*I*magine if the players in a baseball game played according to their own rules. You can't change the rules for following God, either. You don't get to decide what "feels" right to you; God isn't going to change His divine plan to accommodate your whims. God already has a rule book, and He is eager for you to learn His game plan. Don't sit on the sidelines waiting to play.

> *Remember that in a race everyone runs, but only one person gets the prize.*
> *You also must run in such a way that you will win.*
> 1 CORINTHIANS 9:24

_____

_____

_____

_____

_____

THE GOOD, THE BAD, AND THE. . .

*W*e can take comfort in the knowledge that God is involved in our lives. He is aware of every detail, including the stuff we'd just as soon hide from Him. How do you feel about the fact that God knows you completely? If you're like us, it probably gives you a certain amount of fear. That's okay, as long as our fear motivates us to take Him and His commands seriously.

> *"He reveals deep and mysterious things and knows what lies hidden in darkness,*
> *though he himself is surrounded by light."*
> DANIEL 2:22

TYRANNY OF THE STUFF

*T*here is a subtle tyranny that we live under. We have stuff, we accumulate stuff, and it seems that we always want more stuff. God doesn't require that you be an absolute pauper, but He does want you to live free from the tyranny of your stuff. You shouldn't be so enamored with the stuff you have that it interferes with your pursuit of God.

> *Not that I was ever in need, for I have learned how to get along happily whether I have much or little.*
> PHILIPPIANS 4:11

EXPECT TO SUFFER

July 25

*W*hy should any of us expect to get through this life without suffering? If God did not spare His Son from suffering to the point of death, who are we to think that we are exempt? The apostle Paul knew a lot about suffering, and he wrote about it in detail. But he never lost hope, because he knew it was better to suffer for Christ than to live without Him.

In everything we do we try to show that we are true ministers of God.
We patiently endure troubles and hardships and calamities of every kind.
2 CORINTHIANS 6:4

July 26

FOLLOW YOUR LEADERS

*I*n God's paradigm, we are supposed to follow our leaders willingly. Your church leaders are accountable to God for your spiritual welfare. Help them do their job by following their leadership. When you obey them joyfully, you make their job easier and bring honor to God in the process.

Obey your spiritual leaders and do what they say. Their work is to watch over your souls, and they know they are accountable
to God. Give them reason to do this joyfully and not with sorrow. That would certainly not be for your benefit.
HEBREWS 13:17

Don't Let Your Possessions Define You

*F*irst, material possessions are not a measurement of how much God loves you. Second, material possessions aren't related to whether you are a good or a bad person. Finally, your possessions can become a barrier between you and God if you let them. Don't let them interfere with God's plan for your spiritual growth. Try to stay focused on God more than on your goods.

> *Jesus looked around and said to his disciples, "How hard it is for rich people to get into the Kingdom of God!"*
> MARK 10:23

_____

_____

_____

_____

_____

Peace

*T*o the world, the concept of peace means the absence of war. The peace that God offers you is freedom from inner conflict. It doesn't necessarily remove external discord from your circumstances, but it can replace worry and fear. When you have God's peace in your life, you are able to withstand the external discord in your life.

> *"I am leaving you with a gift—peace of mind and heart. And the peace*
> *I give isn't like the peace the world gives. So don't be troubled or afraid."*
> JOHN 14:27

_____

_____

_____

_____

_____

Each New Day

*I*nfuse your life with a little enthusiasm. Focus on the blessings that God has waiting for you each and every day. His love for you never grows stale. He does not become impatient with your spiritual immaturity. His forgiveness continues to be limitless. Instead of being depressed by the repetitiveness of your routine, be excited by the consistency of God's love.

> *Great is his faithfulness; his mercies begin afresh each day.*
> LAMENTATIONS 3:23

God's Book

*O*ne of the most amazing aspects of our relationship with God is that He has given each of us a personal message, and it's one we can read anytime we want. We're talking about the Bible, of course, the greatest book ever written because it is a book written by God. You don't have to wonder about God. You can know about God because He has left you a message. When you read the Bible, it's as if God is talking to you.

> *All Scripture is inspired by God.*
> 2 TIMOTHY 3:16

READ THE INSTRUCTIONS

*I*f you need instructions for a swing set, you certainly need instructions for life. None of us is capable of knowing God and understanding His plans for our lives unless we read His personal instruction book. The Bible isn't a list of dos and don'ts. It's a book of how to do it right. A lot of opinions are floating around, but you can trust the Bible as the standard for testing everything else that claims to be true.

Scripture. . .is useful to teach us what is true.
2 TIMOTHY 3:16

_____
_____
_____
_____
_____

THE TRUTH DETECTOR

*D*on't think of the Bible as a lie detector and God as the guy asking you questions in order to trip you up. The Bible is a truth detector that shows us the right way to live. When we study God's Word and discover for ourselves how He wants us to think and act, we can easily see that anything contrary to God's standard isn't the truth at all.

Scripture. . .is useful. . .to make us realize what is wrong in our lives.
2 TIMOTHY 3:16

_____
_____
_____
_____
_____

STAY ON COURSE

August 2

*A*ll of us need something outside of ourselves and our subjective thinking in order to keep us straight and true. That's why God gave us the Bible. His Word is our plumb line. The Bible is also our compass. There's not much good in staying on course if you don't know where you're going. From the Ten Commandments in the Old Testament to "Love your neighbor as yourself" (Romans 13:9) in the New Testament, the Bible gives practical advice for life.

Scripture. . .straightens us out and teaches us to do what is right.
2 TIMOTHY 3:16

August 3

IN GOD'S DESIGN

*B*eing in God's will doesn't give you a premonition of future events, but it does equip you with the confidence to face whatever circumstances arise. You have the assurance of believing that the One who knows you best and loves you most is directing your life. It means that both the good and bad circumstances can be used as part of God's design to bring you closer to Him.

How do you know what will happen tomorrow? For your life is like the morning fog—
it's here a little while, then it's gone.
JAMES 4:14

Slow the Pace

The Christian life is about relationships, not accomplishments. Most of the time, we are busy scurrying back and forth to work, helping out on committees, and doing errands—in other words, we are occupied with accomplishments. God is love. If you want to reflect God in your life, then you, too, will need to show love. Love must be displayed in the context of relationships with other people.

Stop loving this evil world and all that it offers you, for when you love the world,
you show that you do not have the love of the Father in you.
1 JOHN 2:15

Finish What You Start

Jesus once told a parable about what it means to start something. Whatever it is, we need to see it through, or else we shouldn't start in the first place. The principle applies to material things and relationships, especially our relationship with God. Jesus was very blunt about this. God isn't something to sample and then discard when we lose interest. We are to take Him seriously and believe that when we begin our relationship with Him, we need to see it through.

"Don't begin until you count the cost."
LUKE 14:28

GOD WILL SEE IT THROUGH

God paid such a high price by sending His only Son to die for our sins that He's not about to lose what rightfully belongs to Him. Let the words of Christ give you hope today and the assurance you need tomorrow that God is going to finish what He started.

"I give them eternal life, and they will never perish. No one will snatch them away from me, for my Father has given them to me, and he is more powerful than anyone else. So no one can take them from me."
JOHN 10:28–29

_____

_____

_____

_____

_____

A BALANCED LIFE

Many people are afraid to grow spiritually because they don't want to be stretched. They suspect that the process will involve some awkwardness or discomfort. They don't want to do anything that might make them uncomfortable. Don't be afraid to let God move you along. Don't settle for spiritual stagnation. He is fully able to uphold you in the process of spiritual growth.

God is our refuge and strength, always ready to help in times of trouble.
PSALM 46:1

_____

_____

_____

_____

_____

ANXIETY ADDICTION

*A*nxiety is an unproductive activity. It doesn't accomplish anything positive (although it has plenty of negative effects, such as stress, high blood pressure, and ulcers). You would think that people would try to get rid of their worries if it were possible to do so. And it is! Let God be responsible for the situation. It won't take you twelve steps to get over your anxiety addiction. It takes just one: Give your worries to God.

> *The LORD is good. When trouble comes, he is a strong refuge.*
> *And he knows everyone who trusts in him.*
> NAHUM 1:7

GOD IS RELENTLESS

*G*od is loving, God is forgiving, and God is gracious. But along with His goodness and grace, we have to remember that God is also holy and just. He is pleased with those who give their hearts to Him, but He does not accept the rebellion of those who remain His enemies. God pursues us until we turn to Him, and if we don't, He keeps on coming.

> *The LORD is good. . . . But he sweeps away his enemies in an overwhelming flood.*
> *He pursues his foes into the darkness of night.*
> NAHUM 1:7–8

ADVERSITY

August 10

*A*s long as we live in this world, God doesn't exempt us from the natural consequences of life. But God hasn't left you stranded and helpless. He has given you the Holy Spirit to be His special presence in your life. Consequently, you have all of the spiritual and emotional strength you will need to handle the adversities that life brings your way.

"I have told you all this so that you may have peace in me. Here on earth you will have many trials and sorrows. But take heart, because I have overcome the world."
JOHN 16:33

_____

_____

_____

_____

_____

August 11

SURVIVING CRITICISM

*F*ew things hurt worse than criticism. God is the only One to whom you can go without worrying that you will be criticized. He is the shelter that protects you. While He may not always be pleased with the choices you make, His love for you is unconditional. It is easier to accept criticism when you know that God accepts you.

You hide them in the shelter of your presence, safe from those who conspire against them. You shelter them in your presence, far from accusing tongues.
PSALM 31:20

_____

_____

_____

_____

_____

Dealing with Difficulties

The easiest way to handle difficulties in your life is to change your perspective about them. If God wanted to remove all of the problems from your life, He could. He allows you to go through struggles so you can experience His comfort, His faithfulness, and His presence. It is in problems that your faith brings you closer to God.

Dear brothers and sisters, whenever trouble comes your way, let it be an opportunity for joy.
For when your faith is tested, your endurance has a chance to grow.
JAMES 1:2–3

Facing What's Ahead

Part of the fun of a vacation is the anticipation. But your future isn't filled with vacations. There are uncertainties ahead of you, and they aren't as much fun to anticipate. Don't dwell on what you don't know about the future. Whether your concerns for the future are about finances or relationships or health, trust that God will be there with you when the future happens.

"Don't worry about tomorrow, for tomorrow will bring its own worries."
MATTHEW 6:34

WHAT IS YOUR MOTIVE?

August 14

*H*ow do you please God? By telling others about the good news of Jesus. Even when you tell others about Jesus, you need to examine your motives. How are you approaching people? If you try to convince them by complimenting them or by trying to adapt the good news to their lifestyle, you're not presenting God's message honestly. Jesus never compromised His message by being anything other than a servant.

Never once did we try to win you with flattery, as you very well know.
1 THESSALONIANS 2:5

August 15

ULTIMATE COMFORT

*T*here are plenty of occasions in life when the going is very tough, and you get bumped and bruised by the circumstances of life. You are never too old to turn to your heavenly Father for comfort. Think of Him as standing behind you with His arms outstretched to embrace you. He won't be occupied with something else. He'll pick you up and comfort you.

We who have fled to [God] for refuge can take new courage,
for we can hold on to his promise with confidence.
HEBREWS 6:18

COMPLIMENTS

*Y*ou are wary of insincere friendships, and we don't blame you. So many people bring ulterior motives into a friendship. You can pave the way for meaningful friendships if you dispense with flattery. It creates an atmosphere of insincerity in the relationship. Learn to give compliments that are meaningful and appropriate. A legitimate, sincere compliment shows that you are aware and appreciative of someone else's effort.

God is our witness that we were not just pretending to be your friends so you would give us money!
1 THESSALONIANS 2:5

_____

_____

_____

_____

_____

CHEERFULNESS

*I*f society has a poor impression of Christians, it is no one's fault but our own. We spend too much time being critical, and far too little time being cheerful. We have God on our side to help us through each day, and we know that our future includes an eternity with Him in heaven. You have the knowledge of God in your mind, and you have the love of God in your heart. Make sure your face knows about it.

A cheerful heart is good medicine, but a broken spirit saps a person's strength.
PROVERBS 17:22

_____

_____

_____

_____

_____

SILENCE IS GOLDEN

August 18

*I*f there's one thing we need in the midst of our busy, loud, stressful lives, it's the inner quiet that only God can give. It's the only way to see God's purpose for us. The thing is, God doesn't yell out, "Hey, you're neglecting Me. Sit still for a moment so you can hear Me." Being quiet before God may be one of the hardest things you will ever do. But it may also be the most important.

> *I am silent before you; I won't say a word.*
> PSALM 39:9

THANKFULNESS

August 19

*Y*ou can learn a valuable lesson from the people who never convey their gratitude: Don't be like that. Express your appreciation when someone does something for you. Throughout your entire day, people are engaged in activities that help you in some way. Develop the habit of expressing your gratitude to them.

> *It is good to give thanks to the LORD, to sing praises to the Most High.*
> *It is good to proclaim your unfailing love in the morning, your faithfulness in the evening.*
> PSALM 92:1–2

The Truth about Stories

Great storytellers are great communicators. Jesus Christ, the greatest communicator of all, used stories throughout His ministry on earth. Good stories help you convey and clarify the truth. One of your responsibilities as a Christian is to correctly explain "the word of truth" (2 Timothy 2:15). You can use logic and reasoning to explain the truth, but people aren't always willing to listen to your ideas. However, they will always listen to your stories, especially if they are from your own life.

Here is another story Jesus told. . . .
MATTHEW 13:24

Saying and Doing

Any point that you try to make with words will be disregarded if your actions suggest that you don't believe what you are saying. This principle is particularly true when you talk to other people about God. You take God's reputation with you wherever you go. Make sure that your conduct is consistent with what you have been saying about Him.

Whatever you do or say, let it be as a representative of the Lord Jesus,
all the while giving thanks through him to God the Father.
COLOSSIANS 3:17

KEEP READING

August 22

*E*ffective leaders are eager to gain insights from other sources. This usually means reading books and articles on the subjects that are relevant to their responsibilities. The Bible is the best book for this purpose. It deals with the dynamics of personal relationships, and that is what leadership is all about. If you are in a position of responsibility, make the Bible your leadership manual.

Study this Book of the Law continually. Meditate on it day and night so you
may be sure to obey all that is written in it. Only then will you succeed.
JOSHUA 1:8

_____

_____

_____

_____

_____

August 23

THE GREATEST AUTHOR
IN THE WORLD

*W*e once met one of our favorite authors in person. As exciting as it is to meet an author, the highest privilege we have is to get in touch with the greatest Author in the world. That's right. God is an author, and His book is the world's bestseller. Go ahead. Tell God how much you enjoy His book. We guarantee He will know who you are, and He'll enjoy the experience just as much as you do.

And being made perfect, he became the author of eternal salvation.
HEBREWS 5:9 KJV

_____

_____

_____

_____

_____

NOT TO WORRY

*W*hen you continue to worry about your problems, you are choosing to reject God's offer to comfort you. You are stubbornly holding on to your anxiety and foolishly declining God's help. Either you keep worrying, or you trust God.

> *"Don't worry about having enough food or drink or clothing. . . . Your heavenly Father already knows all your needs, and he will give you all you need from day to day if you live for him and make the Kingdom of God your primary concern."*
> MATTHEW 6:31–33

_____

_____

_____

_____

_____

GOD IS IN THE BIG STUFF

*P*ray for your leaders and do your part to improve your community. If you still have energy after that, ask God to use you to impact the hearts and minds of those who govern you. God has changed the tide of nations before, and there's no reason to believe He won't do it again. Remember, when God's people pray, God listens, and He promises to "heal their land" (2 Chronicles 7:14).

> *There was great joy throughout the land because the LORD had changed the attitude of the king of Assyria toward them.*
> EZRA 6:22

_____

_____

_____

_____

_____

WHAT YOU HAVE ISN'T YOURS

August 26

*A*s the twenty-two-year-old prepared to move out of his parents' home, he looked longingly around the house. Finally, he blurted out, "Why should I leave all of this?" His father was quick to reply, "Because it isn't yours!" Don't ever be stingy with or possessive of what you own. Everything you have is on loan to you from God. Be as generous with your belongings as God would want you to be with His.

The rich and the poor have this in common: The LORD made them both.
PROVERBS 22:2

_____

_____

_____

_____

_____

August 27

SHARING AND HOLDING BACK

*G*od wants us to share our prayer concerns with other believers. But don't dump your self-pity on someone else. When you do that, you're only looking for attention and sympathy. Whenever you are tempted to unload your gripes on someone, resist the urge. Instead, think of what you can say that will be encouraging. They'll benefit from what you have to say.

Though they have been going through much trouble and hard times,
their wonderful joy and deep poverty have overflowed in rich generosity.
2 CORINTHIANS 8:2

_____

_____

_____

_____

_____

IS GOD TOO WEAK?

A forest fire ravaged Yellowstone National Park, and people called it "an act of God." Now that the landscape and animals are back—more beautiful and plentiful than ever—people give the credit to "Mother Nature." Don't buy into that! It is God who blesses His world, down to the tiniest flower (Matthew 6:30). God is powerful enough to save a nation, and He is loving enough to save you.

When our enemies and the surrounding nations heard about it, they were frightened and humiliated.
They realized that this work had been done with the help of our God.
NEHEMIAH 6:16

_____

_____

_____

_____

_____

WHAT MOTIVATES YOU?

W hether it is the clothes you wear, the car you drive, or a brand of deodorant, advertisers have determined that you are motivated by your self-image. Self-image shouldn't be your motivating force if you belong to God. Your motivation should be to please and honor God. Don't get caught as part of the herd that moves according to the dictates of fashion and style. Let God be the One who determines your choices.

"When the Spirit of truth comes, he will guide you into all truth."
JOHN 16:13

_____

_____

_____

_____

_____

MADE FOR A PURPOSE

August 30

Knowing where you came from makes a huge difference in your life. When you know without a doubt that God made the universe and created you in His image (Genesis 1:27), you know you were made for a purpose. Imagine the confidence that gives you! Now move from imagining to believing. Believe that you can live your life on purpose because you were made for a purpose.

We are God's masterpiece. He has created us anew in Christ Jesus,
so that we can do the good things he planned for us long ago.
EPHESIANS 2:10

August 31

CARING IN ACTION

God wants you getting down and dirty as you help others. If you really love God, you're going to get sweaty. Serving Him involves hard work. Maybe God will want you to wash windows or mow the lawn at the home of someone who is ill or disabled. God is more pleased by seeing your dirty hands than your pressed apparel.

Pure and lasting religion in the sight of God our Father means that we must care
for orphans and widows in their troubles, and refuse to let the world corrupt us.
JAMES 1:27

GOD IS PATIENT

*B*ecause God has no other plan than Jesus to bring us into a right relationship with Him, He is willing to wait for us to respond. But God won't wait forever. He has chosen the best possible moment to send Jesus back to earth. When that happens, time—like God's patience—will finally run out.

The Lord isn't really being slow about his promise to return, as some people think. No, he is being patient for your sake. He does not want anyone to perish, so he is giving more time for everyone to repent.
2 PETER 3:9

_____

_____

_____

_____

_____

GREATNESS

*T*here is nothing wrong with doing something for someone who can reciprocate. But there is nothing great about it, either. Don't think that you have the attitude of a humble servant when you offer to do a favor for someone if you have a "Now he owes me one" mentality. Look for things that you can do for someone who has no ability to repay you. When you aren't concerned about keeping things equal, then you'll be acting like a humble servant.

"Anyone who welcomes a little child like this on my behalf is welcoming me."
MATTHEW 18:5

_____

_____

_____

_____

_____

THE DANGER OF KNOWLEDGE

September 3

*Y*ou'll never come to the point where you know enough about God. Knowing God is a lifelong pursuit that grows more rewarding as you learn more. Learning about God brings you peace, joy, and a desire to know God better. Don't substitute what you know about God objectively for actually knowing God personally. He belongs in your heart, where He can change you into the person He wants you to be, reflecting His glory to others.

Fear of the LORD is the beginning of knowledge.
PROVERBS 1:7

September 4

HANDLING MONEY

*M*oney can involve a vicious cycle. Don't get caught in it. If you feel compelled to match the acquisitions of your friends and neighbors, you will be in a race that has no finish line. Let God help you establish an acceptable standard of living for your circumstances. If He gives you financial blessings, think about giving away the excess before you automatically spend it on yourself.

Don't weary yourself trying to get rich. Why waste your time?
For riches can disappear as though they had the wings of a bird!
PROVERBS 23:4–5

An Offer You Can't Refuse

*W*hat would you do if God offered you anything you wanted? How did Solomon respond? He asked for "an understanding mind" (I Kings 3:9). To say God answered his request is an understatement. History records that Solomon was the wisest man who ever lived. He will give you wisdom if you ask for it. As you gain wisdom, you will begin to see things from God's perspective.

> *If you need wisdom—if you want to know what God wants you to do—ask him, and he will gladly tell you.*
> JAMES 1:5

_____

_____

_____

_____

_____

What Is Your Response-Ability?

*P*erspective is everything. Look at circumstances from God's point of view. If you have an eternal perspective, then all of your difficulties will seem to shrink. God doesn't see insurmountable obstacles in your life, although they may appear that way to you. He is able to conquer any adverse situation, so look at it through His eyes. Before you know it, the problem will be gone, and the unpleasantness will be forgotten.

> *Yet I will rejoice in the LORD! I will be joyful in the God of my salvation.*
> HABAKKUK 3:18

_____

_____

_____

_____

_____

THE RIGHT THING

September 7

*O*ne dictionary definition of *wisdom* is "knowledge and good judgment based on experience." That sounds good, but what if your experiences aren't so good? Here's Solomon's advice: "Fear of the Lord is the beginning of wisdom" (Proverbs 9:10). As Chuck Swindoll says, to fear God means to "take Him seriously and do what He says." When you do what God says, you do what's right. And when you do what's right, you are wise.

Those who are wise will find a time and a way to do what is right.
ECCLESIASTES 8:5

September 8

WHAT IS REALLY FUNNY?

*W*e all like to make people laugh. It is rewarding to bring levity into someone's life. Unfortunately, some people try too hard to be funny. In their attempt, they go for the "cheap shot" instead of a humorous comment. Christians should be the happiest group of people. They should be laughing often. But their jokes should never be made at the expense of someone's feelings.

Be kind to each other, tenderhearted, forgiving one another, just as God through Christ has forgiven you.
EPHESIANS 4:32

Spiritual Discernment

*A*s a Christian you have spiritual discernment, thanks to the presence of the Holy Spirit in your life (1 Corinthians 2:12). Now, it's possible for people without God to be wise in the ways of the world, but when it comes to spiritual matters, they are in a fog (1 Corinthians 2:14). As long as you ask God for wisdom, you will accomplish amazing things for God.

> *If you just listen and don't obey, it is like looking at your face in a mirror*
> *but doing nothing to improve your appearance.*
> JAMES 1:23

Prayer Prevails

September 10

*W*orry usually results when you have exhausted all of your options. Don't withhold your prayers until everything else fails. Your first step in tackling a problem should be to pray about it. But you'll never hit the proverbial brick wall if you remember to pray your way through it. When you talk to God, He'll give you peace in the midst of your problems, and you'll be better able to keep working through the challenge.

> *Don't worry about anything; instead, pray about everything.*
> *Tell God what you need, and thank him for all he has done.*
> PHILIPPIANS 4:6

SIDE BY SIDE

September 11

*O*ne of the best ways to communicate with someone is to walk side by side. That's the picture of how God relates to us. He sent Jesus to die for us, but after He rose from the dead, Jesus returned to heaven, where He is on our side pleading for us before the Father (1 John 2:1). And right here on earth, the Holy Spirit comes alongside us as our Counselor and Comforter (John 14:16).

"I will ask the Father, and he will give you another Counselor, who will never leave you."
JOHN 14:16

September 12

DISGUISED GOSSIP

*Y*ou wouldn't schedule a weekly meeting at Starbucks with a few friends for a gossip session. But there is a risk that the same thing could happen with as much regularity at many churches. We're talking about "prayer meetings." There is temptation to gossip when you are sharing "prayer requests" about other people. Satan knows that prayers are effective. He will try to get you distracted from thoughts of God's sovereignty and focused more on people's scandal.

What dainty morsels rumors are—but they sink deep into one's heart.
PROVERBS 26:22

ARE YOU PREJUDICED?

*P*rejudice is the barrier that keeps one person from accepting another. Jesus was unaffected by racial, social, and cultural barriers. He wanted to share His message about God's love with everyone. That's why He ignored social differences and began talking with the Samaritan woman, who not only had a bad reputation but was also a member of a despised race (John 4:4–26). See people through the eyes of Jesus, as those who need to know God's love.

Doesn't this discrimination show that you are guided by wrong motives?
JAMES 2:4

WHAT'S YOUR CHOICE?

*E*ternity is serious business, because it never ends. Where you will spend eternity is your own choice. If you haven't made up your mind yet, here is a thought that might be of help: For Christians, life on this earth is as close as they will ever get to hell. For people who reject God, life on this earth is as close as they will ever get to heaven.

"Everyone who believes in me will have eternal life."
JOHN 3:15

God Isn't in Our Image

September 15

The Bible tells us that God created people in His image. What if God acted like people do? We should thank God that He isn't in our image. He doesn't lie, He doesn't change, He doesn't judge unfairly, and He doesn't love conditionally. He is God, and above Him there is no other.

"God is not a man, that he should lie. He is not a human, that he should change his mind.
Has he ever spoken and failed to act?
Has he ever promised and not carried it through?"
NUMBERS 23:19

_____

_____

_____

_____

_____

September 16

Diversity

Diversity was an issue in the first-century churches. Early Christian churches were composed of Jews and Gentiles, the rich and the slaves, the educated and the illiterate. In the context of these widespread differences, Paul urged unity. Paul's message isn't limited to individual churches. It applies to all believers, among whom there will be significant diversity in worship styles and the formality of their respective services. If we learn to value each other as God sees us, our differences will not be divisive.

Always keep yourselves united in the Holy Spirit, and bind yourselves together with peace.
EPHESIANS 4:3

_____

_____

_____

_____

_____

Do God's Thing

We humans have a history of doing our own thing, usually with disastrous results. It's called rebellion against God. When people reject God's way of doing things and choose their own, they reject a perfect plan in favor of a corrupt path. Every day we are faced with choices, most of which come back to the same question: Do we want to do things our way or God's way?

In those days Israel had no king, so the people did whatever seemed right in their own eyes.
JUDGES 17:6

_____

_____

_____

_____

_____

Faults

It is easier to see the faults in other people. We can quickly identify the problems in someone else's life. Nobody is perfect. But if you are interested in honing your critical skills, you should start with yourself. Don't move on to others until you have completely identified all of your shortcomings and corrected each of them.

"Hypocrite! First get rid of the log from your own eye; then perhaps you will see well enough to deal with the speck in your friend's eye."
MATTHEW 7:5

_____

_____

_____

_____

_____

WORD POWER

September 19

*W*ords are amazingly versatile. They can be destructive weapons, or they can be agents of peace. Every day we make choices as to how we are going to use our words, or at least we should. It's not just a matter of thinking before we speak. We need to build our vocabulary to include those words that edify and encourage others. The negative words come all too naturally (because those are mainly what we hear), but positive words take work.

Kind words are like honey—sweet to the soul and healthy for the body.
PROVERBS 16:24

September 20

A GOOD INVESTMENT

A good investment is determined by the safety of your capital and the rate of return. These same principles apply to the investment of your time and energy. You may receive the best return on your investment when you put time into other people. You can invest in them through acts of kindness and thoughtfulness.

Don't just pretend that you love others. Really love them. Hate what is wrong. Stand on the side of the good. Love each other with genuine affection, and take delight in honoring each other.
ROMANS 12:9–10

GUARD YOUR HEART

*I*f all you had to worry about was keeping your physical body healthy, then you could concentrate completely on the food you put into your mouth. But your body has a spiritual dimension, as well, and you can easily feed it with unhealthful sights and sounds. Above all else, guard your ears and your eyes. Just as your mouth is the gateway to your body, they are the gateways to your heart.

> *"Your eye is a lamp for your body. A pure eye lets sunshine into your soul."*
> MATTHEW 6:22

_____

_____

_____

_____

_____

WHAT'S LEFT AFTER DEATH?

*Y*our tombstone is likely to be engraved with the year of your birth and the year of your death. But the impact of your life is not relegated to the etchings on a tombstone. The heritage that you leave behind will be the influence you had on others. Leave them an example of a life committed to God. Let your legacy be a reverence for God.

> *I could have no greater joy than to hear that my children live in the truth.*
> 3 JOHN 4

_____

_____

_____

_____

_____

LIVING THE TRUTH

*I*t is easy to get so accustomed to religious lingo that we forget what it really means. For example, we use a phrase such as "living in the light" without remembering its significance. Meditate on the meaning of what you read in scripture. What you read should change the way you think. How you think should change the way you live.

> *If we are living in the light of God's presence, just as Christ is, then we have fellowship with each other,*
> *and the blood of Jesus, his Son, cleanses us from every sin.*
> 1 JOHN 1:7

_____

_____

_____

_____

_____

YOU ARE GOD'S HOUSE

*I*n a very real spiritual sense, you are a "house of God." You begin your relationship with God by inviting Jesus into your house. Once you invite Jesus in, the Holy Spirit takes up residence in your body, which is like a "temple" for God (1 Corinthians 6:19). You are the house of God, and as long as He is going to live there, He expects you to take care of His place.

> *"Why are you living in luxurious houses while my house lies in ruins?"*
> HAGGAI 1:4

_____

_____

_____

_____

_____

Family Ties

September 25

*W*e live in a society where it is easy to become disconnected from family. It seems that the farther we live from each other, the more distant our relationships become. But there doesn't have to be a proportional relationship between distance and family connectedness. Take advantage of the Internet and send e-mail messages to your family members regularly. Stay in touch with family. They need to know you care.

Those who won't care for their own relatives, especially those living in the same household,
have denied what we believe. Such people are worse than unbelievers.
1 TIMOTHY 5:8

The Love of Money

September 26

*T*here are many things you should pray for, but money isn't one of them. Pray for God's provision, but don't pray for riches. The problem isn't money but our desire for it. Friendships end, marriages break apart, crimes are committed, and people stay away from God—all over money. Money is a weak spot for us, and Satan knows it. That's why you need to count on the almighty God to help you keep your eyes on Him.

"You cannot serve both God and money."
LUKE 16:13

THE LURE OF SEX

*A*ll sin is equally bad in God's eyes. However, we may be more susceptible to sexual sin than other sins because it can invade our thoughts as well as our bodies (Matthew 5:28). God designed sex for marriage, and anything else degrades your relationship with Him. It infects your thoughts and lessens the effectiveness of the Holy Spirit in your life. That's why God doesn't want us to be passive about sexual temptation.

Run away from sexual sin! No other sin so clearly affects the body as this one does.
1 CORINTHIANS 6:18

THE LONGING FOR POWER

*T*he last of the "big three" temptations is power. If anyone was immune to the temptation of power, it was Jesus. Yet that's exactly where Satan tempted Him. He offered Jesus the world if Jesus would kneel down and worship him (Matthew 4:9). Satan used that tactic on Jesus, and you can be sure he will use it on you. Tell Satan to take a hike, and rely on the Word of God.

"Get out of here, Satan," Jesus told him. "For the Scriptures say,
'You must worship the Lord your God; serve only him.'"
MATTHEW 4:10

Friendships Fit Together

The value of friendship is more than a matter of convenience. It is a matter of completeness. Your friends can complement your weak areas. Although you have much in common with your friends, they will have perspectives and opinions that are different from yours. Take time to thank the Lord for your friends. Then call a few of your friends and thank them for their friendship.

A person standing alone can be attacked and defeated, but two can stand back-to-back and conquer.
Three are even better, for a triple-braided cord is not easily broken.
ECCLESIASTES 4:12

What to Do with What You Hear

It is a constant struggle to keep your mind on the things of God. If you hear a personal criticism, don't overreact. While some of the comment may be false, it just might contain a shred of truth. And if you hear a criticism of someone else, don't dwell on it. When your mind strays, refocus on God.

Fix your thoughts on what is true and honorable and right. Think about things that are pure
and lovely and admirable. Think about things that are excellent and worthy of praise.
PHILIPPIANS 4:8

REJECT REJECTION

October 1

*H*ere's a way to get out of the ugly cycle of judgment and rejection. Whenever you meet people, try to see them the way Jesus does. See others as people Jesus loves so much that He died for them. If you begin to see people in this way, not only will you accept them, but you may also be used by God to share the good news of His love with them.

> *Yes indeed, it is good when you truly obey our Lord's royal command found in the Scriptures: "Love your neighbor as yourself."*
> JAMES 2:8

October 2

PRIDE

A prideful spirit has you looking at yourself instead of looking up toward God. Pride in ourselves, in our possessions, or in our accomplishments is a slap in God's face. Our pride means that we are taking credit for what God has given us. Instead of being prideful, we should be humble before God and grateful for His mercy to us.

> *If we are living now by the Holy Spirit, let us follow the Holy Spirit's leading in every part of our lives. Let us not become conceited.*
> GALATIANS 5:25–26

FALSELY ACCUSED

*B*eing falsely accused is difficult to handle. In fact, it may be one of the most difficult personal obstacles you will ever face. When others try to discredit you, are you willing to let God defend you? If you are falsely accused and suffer for doing right, don't assume you are the only one who can protect and defend your reputation. Do what Jesus did and trust that God will take care of the situation.

> *For we know the one who said, "I will take vengeance. I will repay those who deserve it."*
> HEBREWS 10:30

SPECIAL FAVOR

*J*esus did more than show us a better way to live. By sacrificing His life for us, He did us a "special favor." He made it possible for us to satisfy God's perfect standard by His forgiveness rather than by our own performance. Don't think that by doing everything right, you'll be good enough for God. You can't do it. Your lifestyle should be in response to God's love, not an attempt to win His love.

> *"We believe that we are all saved the same way, by the special favor of the Lord Jesus."*
> ACTS 15:11

THE SIMPLE LIFE

*Q*uick riches never did anyone any good. They certainly never brought anyone happiness. We've never heard anyone say, "I'm rich, and finally I'm happy." Instead, we've heard comments such as "Wealth is a burden" or "I wish my life were a lot simpler." There's nothing wrong with wealth (and neither is there any dishonor in poverty). What matters is your contentment with what you have.

We are merely moving shadows, and all our busy rushing ends in nothing. We heap up wealth for someone else to spend.
PSALM 39:6

NO WORRIES

*W*orry isn't only a verb; it's an emotion. We think that if we worry enough, our circumstances are going to change. We think we can worry things and events into existence. When we worry, we make a choice not to trust God. God has made it clear that He is very interested in us and very capable of helping us. Give your cares and problems to God.

Give all your worries and cares to God, for he cares about what happens to you.
1 PETER 5:7

PREPARING FOR BATTLE

*A*s a Christian, you are engaged in a spiritual battle. Satan is doing everything he can to prevent you from living a victorious life. God has provided battle gear for your protection and weapons for your use. Read about spiritual armor in Ephesians 6:10–18. Notice that there is no protection for your back. With God on your side, you will never have to run away from Satan in defeat.

> *Put on all of God's armor so that you will be able to stand firm against all strategies and tricks of the Devil.*
> EPHESIANS 6:11

HANDLING TEMPTATION

*T*here is nothing wrong with temptation. Until you give in to it, you haven't done anything wrong. You'll never resist temptation if you try to do it in your own power. It will happen only with God's power through the Holy Spirit. Depend on God for the power to resist. Focus on Him instead of the temptation.

> *God is faithful. He will keep the temptation from becoming so strong that you can't stand up against it. When you are tempted, he will show you a way out so that you will not give in to it.*
> 1 CORINTHIANS 10:13

IF NOT US, WHO?

October 9

It was no accident when a beautiful Jewish woman named Esther became queen of Persia. God arranged the circumstances of her life. Whenever you are promoted to a higher position, you need to recognize that God has put you there for a reason. You have to trust God that His timing is perfect, and you need to stay humble with the knowledge that He wants to use you to glorify Him.

> *"What's more, who can say but that you have been elevated to the palace for just such a time as this?"*
> ESTHER 4:14

YOUR VALUES

October 10

God is calling you to live according to His principles, but they are of a higher level than society's rules and values. Society's principles stop at your door and allow you to do whatever you want in your private life. That's not the way it is in God's plan. He wants you to live according to His holiness.

> *God has called us to be holy, not to live impure lives. Anyone who refuses to live by these rules*
> *is not disobeying human rules but is rejecting God, who gives his Holy Spirit to you.*
> I THESSALONIANS 4:7–8

DREAM ON

It's in our nature to dream. Let's talk about your daydreams for a minute. One big dream every Christian should have centers on the stuff God has prepared for us beyond this life on earth (1 Corinthians 2:9). This is not a fantasy land. Heaven is for real. This truth should give you tremendous motivation to serve God on earth and love Him with your whole being.

> *What is faith? It is the confident assurance that what we hope for is going to happen.*
> *It is the evidence of things we cannot yet see.*
> HEBREWS 11:1

_____

_____

_____

_____

_____

TALK ABOUT FOREVER

Heaven is a very real place that Jesus is preparing for those who believe in Him. The Bible makes it clear that unbelievers have a very different future. The descriptions of hell as a "lake of fire" and a "place of torment" give us a clue that it will be a terrible place. Since Christ died to keep people out of hell, can't you make some effort to talk with your friends and family about this most important choice?

> *"Their doom is in the lake that burns with fire and sulfur. This is the second death."*
> REVELATION 21:8

_____

_____

_____

_____

_____

GOD WILL NEVER LEAVE YOU

October 13

*O*ne of the greatest fears we have is abandonment. As an adult, you don't fear being abandoned physically as much as you hate the idea of emotional abandonment. You may even feel as though God has abandoned you at times. When those feelings of abandonment come, rest on the promises of God's Word.

The Lord does not abandon anyone forever. Though he brings grief, he also shows compassion according to the greatness of his unfailing love. For he does not enjoy hurting people or causing them sorrow.
LAMENTATIONS 3:31–33

October 14

HUMILITY

*H*umility is subtle. The moment you think you have it, you've lost it. A spirit of arrogance is at odds with godly living. You can move toward humility if you remain submissive to God's leading. If you need a picture of humility, think of Christ. It was a supreme act of humility for Him to take on human form when He was God's own Son.

"God sets himself against the proud, but he shows favor to the humble." So humble yourselves under the mighty power of God, and in his good time he will honor you.
1 PETER 5:5–6

START TRUSTING

*W*orry is a double-edged sword. Not only is worry incapable of adding anything good to your life, it can also take things away from your life. Worry leads to stress, which damages you physically. The time you spend worrying takes away from the time you spend doing other things. When you spend less time doing other things, your productivity drops. The only way to add to your life is to stop worrying and start trusting.

"Can all your worries add a single moment to your life? Of course not."
MATTHEW 6:27

_____

_____

_____

_____

_____

MERCY

*B*ecause we have violated God's perfect standard, we have been declared guilty and there's nothing we can do about it. We're at the mercy of the Judge of heaven. God showed us His mercy by sending His Son to take the punishment we deserved. The next time you feel like retaliating against someone who has offended you, remember the mercy that God extended to you.

*That is why God had mercy on me, so that Christ Jesus could use me
as a prime example of his great patience with even the worst sinners.*
I TIMOTHY 1:16

_____

_____

_____

_____

_____

GOD WANTS YOUR PROBLEMS

*J*ust about every problem you worry about is outside your control, which gives you the perfect opportunity to give your problems to God. At their worst, problems cause us to worry. At their best, problems test our faith. Do we trust God enough to let Him control everything in our lives? Are we willing to give Him our big problems as well as the small stuff? He's willing to take control of our difficulties if we just let Him.

God will use this persecution to show his justice.
2 THESSALONIANS 1:5

FINDING A TRUE FRIEND

*W*hen you were young, you didn't have much choice about your friends. Even as you got older, your friends at school were determined in large part by the classes you had. You are now at a stage when you get to select your own friends. Don't let it happen by default. Be very intentional about it. Look for friends who will raise you up to a higher level; avoid the people who would pull you down to theirs.

As iron sharpens iron, a friend sharpens a friend.
PROVERBS 27:17

THE WORRY SUBSTITUTE

*I*t's hard to stop worrying. Even though the habit is harmful to you, you can't help but engage in the activity. So what's the best way to stop? You can't just turn off your worry like you turn off a faucet. The Expert says you need to substitute prayer. When you get an urge to worry, pray.

> *He will be gracious if you ask for help. He will respond instantly to the sound of your cries.*
> ISAIAH 30:19

SPIRITUAL GROWTH

October 20

*S*piritual growth doesn't happen all at once. It is a lifelong process. First of all, we continue to live in a sinful world, so we'll never be perfect in our lifetime. Second, we continually find ourselves in new situations. Third, we gain a greater understanding of God as we learn to depend on Him. Finally, spiritual growth doesn't happen all at once because there is so much to learn about God.

> *The more you grow like this, the more you will become productive and useful in your knowledge of our Lord Jesus Christ.*
> 2 PETER 1:8

October 21

COMFORT OTHERS

*T*here are things God gives us that He expects us to give to others. Forgiveness is one of those things (Matthew 6:14). God loves us, and He expects us to love others (1 John 4:11). God also comforts us, and He expects us to comfort others. If God has given you a lot of comfort in your life, it means you have done a lot of suffering. Now use your experiences to help relieve the suffering of others.

I would speak in a way that helps you. I would try to take away your grief.
JOB 16:5

_____

_____

_____

_____

_____

October 22

PREPARE NOW FOR ETERNITY

*W*ere you one of those kids who procrastinated in school? The moment of truth comes when the comment on the report card reads, "Does not make good use of time." That would be a terrible remark for God to make about us. He has given us a limited amount of time to work for His kingdom. We have exactly until we die or until Christ returns. Make good use of the time God has given you.

Make the most of every opportunity for doing good in these evil days.
EPHESIANS 5:16

_____

_____

_____

_____

_____

God in You

Christians should be the most enthusiastic people of all, because they have God in their lives. If you have doubts about this, just look at the word "enthusiasm." It comes from two Greek words: *en*, meaning "in," and *theos*, which is the word for "God." In other words, *enthusiasm* means "God in you." When God is in your life and you know He is working in everything you do, you can't help but be enthusiastic.

It was your enthusiasm that stirred up many of them to begin helping.
2 CORINTHIANS 9:2

Talk about Others

October 24

When you talk to others, talk about others (and we're not talking gossip here). Ask them questions. Find out what they think and what makes them tick. Don't worry about stating your opinion. When you show interest in others, others find you interesting, and it's only a matter of time before they want to know what makes you tick.

"The proud will be humbled, but the humble will be honored."
LUKE 18:14

THANKING GOD

*W*e too often take for granted the fact that God is always with us. Make it a regular part of your life to thank the Lord for His continuing mercies. Mealtime is a great way to remember. Since you remember to eat several times a day, you can take those opportunities to spend a minute or two acknowledging God's importance in your life.

"When you go through deep waters and great trouble, I will be with you. . . .
When you walk through the fire of oppression, you will not be burned up; the flames will not consume you."
ISAIAH 43:2

_____

_____

_____

_____

_____

MAKE SOMEONE HAPPY

*H*appiness may be temporary, but we all want it. Here's another thing we need to realize about happiness: It's harder to come by when we derive it from things. A better way to gain happiness is to do things for others. Make others happy, and the happiest person will be you. Make others happy all the time, and your happiness will turn to joy.

I hope to visit you soon and to talk with you face to face. Then our joy will be complete.
2 JOHN 12

_____

_____

_____

_____

_____

GLORIFY GOD

Why did God create us in the first place? God wants us to glorify Him. The meaning of glory is "gift," literally a gift of honor and praise. In everything we do, God wants us to glorify Him. According to the Westminster Confession of Faith, our "chief and highest end is to glorify God, and fully to enjoy Him forever." That's what happens when you honor God and give Him praise. You enjoy Him forever.

Whatever you eat or drink or whatever you do, you must do all for the glory of God.
1 CORINTHIANS 10:31

LOYALTY

Acquaintances are people you know. They pop into your life as the result of your circumstances. One of the characteristics that distinguishes acquaintanceship from friendship is loyalty. Friends are committed to each other. They are willing to make personal sacrifices for each other. If you have true friends, then thank God for them. If you need to increase your friendship network and find a few, then start by being the kind of friend you would want to have.

"The greatest love is shown when people lay down their lives for their friends."
JOHN 15:13

LEADERSHIP

October 29

*G*od notices leaders, God watches leaders, and God expects a lot out of leaders. The reason, we suspect, is that leaders are more responsible for others than followers are. We're not saying that followers don't have responsibilities, too, but leaders have a greater responsibility to demonstrate wisdom, respect, and integrity.

> *"Much is required from those to whom much is given, and much more is required from those to whom much more is given."*
> LUKE 12:48

October 30

THE BEST SUCCESS FORMULA

*H*ere is a success formula as timeless as God Himself: "Repent and be saved." Now we admit that you are more likely to see this formula on a street preacher's sign than on the cover of a self-help book. It doesn't exactly inspire you to go out there and make something of yourself. What God wants you to do is ask Him to make you successful.

> *Beg the LORD to save you—all you who are humble, all you who uphold justice. Walk humbly and do what is right.*
> ZEPHANIAH 2:3

What Happens in You

*M*onitoring changes in your schedule is important, but it is not as important as monitoring the changes in your heart. Don't forget that changes should be happening inside of you, as well. We're referring to the strengthening of your character as you grow closer to God. Spend as much time today thinking about your character as you spend planning your calendar.

> *The LORD has already told you what is good, and this is what he requires:*
> *to do what is right, to love mercy, and to walk humbly with your God.*
> MICAH 6:8

_____

_____

_____

_____

_____

You Aren't Lucky

November 1

*W*hen something good happens, we often say, "Well, that was lucky." We must understand that nothing in our lives and in our world happens outside of God's knowledge and control. He loves us completely and would never do anything to harm us. Anything good that happens to you is not because you are lucky or fortunate. Luck is powerless to do anything. God is the One who gives you all good things.

> *Whatever is good and perfect comes to us from God above, who created all heaven's lights.*
> JAMES 1:17

_____

_____

_____

_____

_____

RELY ON GOD'S PERSPECTIVE

November 2

Since God is sovereign and in control of all things, it's difficult to understand why He allows some things to happen to us. Let's remind ourselves that God's personality traits include love and omniscience. He cannot do anything that is not in the best interests of His children. We may not understand it, but we can trust that He knows what He is doing.

We know that God causes everything to work together for the good of those who love God and are called according to his purpose for them.
ROMANS 8:28

November 3

SEASONS OF LIFE

Just as there are seasons in nature, there are seasons in life. Spring is the season of joy, when new growth occurs. Summer is made for relaxing, vacationing, and renewing. Fall can lull you into complacency. You may even take God for granted. Winter is the time when you need God more than ever, even though He seems far away. Call out to God, and He will answer by giving you the strength to get through it.

There is a time for everything, a season for every activity under heaven.
ECCLESIASTES 3:1

WHAT KIND OF WORKER ARE YOU?

*I*f you belong to God, and if other people know it, they will be evaluating God by what they see in you. This means you need to work diligently and excellently at your assigned tasks. Few things leave a worse impression than a job left unfinished or a job poorly done.

We are God's masterpiece. He has created us anew in Christ Jesus,
so that we can do the good things he planned for us long ago.
EPHESIANS 2:10

THE HEART TELLS ALL

*I*n a culture obsessed with money and possessions, God's people need to constantly evaluate their definition of success. We need to make sure we aren't following the culture by making our stuff the measure of our success. Your heart will follow whatever is most important to you. If it's money, that's where your heart will be. If it's putting God and others first, then your heart will show it.

Those who love money will never have enough. How absurd to think that wealth brings true happiness!
ECCLESIASTES 5:10

HAVE A GOOD HEART

November 6

*J*esus said that you can tell what is in a person's heart by listening to what that person says. He used the word *heart* to mean a person's true character and feelings. You can easily guess the character of a person whose words are encouraging, kind, and truthful. People can't see your heart, but they can see (and hear) what your heart produces.

"A good person produces good words from a good heart, and an evil person produces evil words from an evil heart."
MATTHEW 12:35

November 7

A TEACHABLE SPIRIT

*E*ven if you complete your formal schooling, plan to keep learning. Your "lifetime learning" will come from many sources. We predict you'll enjoy reaching deeper levels of understanding as you learn from and about God. Secondarily, you can learn a lot about yourself from your friends. There is a lot left to learn if you are willing to be teachable.

Let those who are wise understand these things. Let those who are discerning listen carefully.
The paths of the LORD are true and right, and righteous people live by walking in them.
HOSEA 14:9

Two Natures—Two Results

As a Christian, you can choose to live in your own power, which the Bible calls "the old sinful nature." Or you can choose to live "according to your new life in the Holy Spirit" (Galatians 5:16). If that's your choice, here are the results of the Spirit's power in your life: "love, joy, peace, patience, kindness, goodness, faithfulness, gentleness, and self-control" (Galatians 5:22–23).

> *I advise you to live according to your new life in the Holy Spirit. Then you won't be doing what your sinful nature craves.*
> GALATIANS 5:16

A Family Resemblance

If you want people to know that you belong to God, your "family resemblance" should be godliness. That trait might look like this in your life: knowing the truth—which comes from studying God's Word; acting with integrity—which comes from doing God's Word; and living with passion—which comes from sharing God's Word. If you have these characteristics, people will easily see the family resemblance between you and your heavenly Father.

> *All will be well for those who are godly. Tell them, "You will receive a wonderful reward!"*
> ISAIAH 3:10

DON'T TAKE PITY

November 10

It's easy to take pity on others, but we should never offer our help out of pity. You feel sorry for them, but you keep them at arm's length. By contrast, compassion gets you involved emotionally as well as financially. Your heart "goes out" to the people who are helpless, so you respond generously, knowing that your money is useful but is hardly a substitute for the real work you must do.

You are generous because of your faith.
PHILEMON 6

_____
_____
_____
_____
_____

November 11

BE WISE IN YOUR COMPASSION

When it comes to generosity, there are two questions to ask. First, does it come from your heart? If your motive isn't right, then it doesn't matter how much you give away. Second, is your generosity productive? As a Christian, you are called to a higher standard so that your giving can make a difference. Don't just hope the organizations use your money wisely. Hold them and yourself accountable by getting involved, thereby multiplying your investment in God's work.

I am praying that you will really put your generosity to work, for in so doing you
will come to an understanding of all the good things we can do for Christ.
PHILEMON 6

_____
_____
_____
_____
_____

TRUE CHARITY

*L*et God direct your charitable decisions. You need to rely on His guidance for when, how much, and to whom your gifts should be made. Sometimes you'll need to give when no tax deduction is available (such as paying the car repair bill for a friend who has been laid off work). Other times, you may need to give cash anonymously.

> *You must each make up your own mind as to how much you should give. Don't give*
> *reluctantly or in response to pressure. For God loves the person who gives cheerfully.*
> 2 CORINTHIANS 9:7

ALWAYS ENOUGH

*E*lijah depended on the generosity of others for just about every material need, but when God sent him to a poor widow, he had to wonder. Yet an amazing thing happened. As the widow gave Elijah what little food she had, there was always enough food left over for her and her son. That's the way it is with generous people. They don't get rich because of their generosity, but they always seem to have enough.

> *No matter how much they used, there was always enough left in the containers, just as the LORD had promised.*
> 1 KINGS 17:16

THE TWO SIDES OF GOSSIP

*G*ossip is bad—always and totally. But the people who do it—the gossips—are only half of the problem. The other half of the blame must be laid on the people who listen to the gossip. If everyone refused to listen to gossip, the problem would be solved. Since your ears can't close by themselves, using your feet can help. Just walk away whenever you overhear gossip.

A troublemaker plants seeds of strife; gossip separates the best of friends.
PROVERBS 16:28

GIVE GLORY TO GOD

*T*here's a difference between doing things for God in order to impress others and doing things for God in order to impress God! When your motive is to impress others, your good deeds—the ones God wants you to do—are going to bring attention to you. When your motive is to impress and please God, that changes everything. He gets the glory. God wants us to shine the light on Him so everyone can see.

"Let your good deeds shine out for all to see, so that everyone will praise your heavenly Father."
MATTHEW 5:16

An Affordable Lifestyle

The obvious drawback to borrowing money is the fact that you have to pay it back. When the due date approaches, the stress increases. Debt demands your attention. You'll find few spare moments to be meditating on God if you're constantly worried about the next monthly payment. It is difficult to see God when you are buried in debt. Avoid getting into excessive debt. Adjust your lifestyle so you can manage with the money you have.

Just as the rich rule the poor, so the borrower is servant to the lender.
PROVERBS 22:7

A New Heart

Are there people whose hearts are hardened against God today? Absolutely. All of us start out with a hardened heart. Every one of us is turned against God, and we remain that way until we turn our hearts over to God. God promises to replace our hard hearts with hearts that follow after Him. God also gives us the Holy Spirit so that our hearts will never harden again.

"I will give you a new heart with new and right desires, and I will put a new spirit in you."
EZEKIEL 36:26

PRAISE

*D*id you know that God loves to be praised? Here are two reasons we need to praise God. First, He should be honored. He is so magnificent that He deserves it. Second, we need to thank Him constantly because it reminds us that what we have comes from Him. Spend time praising Him for who He is and what He has already done for you.

> *All honor to the God and Father of our Lord Jesus Christ, for it is by his*
> *boundless mercy that God has given us the privilege of being born again.*
> 1 PETER 1:3

STAY STRONG AND SWIFT

*F*ew people take Satan seriously, because he's the funny guy with the horns and a pitchfork. What if Satan's image was more like that of a lion? Just like the lion, Satan seeks to attack the weak and the stragglers in the herd. He preys on the feeble and the slow. To keep Satan off your back, stay strong and swift in the Lord.

> *Be careful! Watch out for attacks from the Devil, your great enemy.*
> *He prowls around like a roaring lion, looking for some victim to devour.*
> 1 PETER 5:8

STICK WITH IT

*E*verything that's worthwhile in life requires perseverance. That's especially true of living as a Christ-follower. Yet even as you persevere, you must realize that you can't run and finish this marathon race called the Christian life alone. You need Jesus, who not only saved you but also helps you right now in your struggle against discouragement and sin.

> *Let us run with endurance the race that God has set before us. We do this by*
> *keeping our eyes on Jesus, on whom our faith depends from start to finish.*
> HEBREWS 12:1–2

RIGHTS VERSUS RESPONSIBILITIES

November 21

*R*ights are all about "me, me, me." That is not the attitude God wants you to have. He wants you to forget about your rights and focus on your responsibilities. He wants you fully engaged in helping others. Responsibilities are all about "you, you, you." Most people want to be served and enjoy their privileges. God calls us to be submissive and put the interests of others above our own.

> *Your attitude should be the same that Christ Jesus had. Though he was God,*
> *he did not demand and cling to his rights as God.*
> PHILIPPIANS 2:5–6

A Grateful Heart

November 22

*S*ervice is big these days. A lot of companies have built their reputations on service, so we have come to expect it. Sometimes it is necessary to correct a wrong, but most of our ranting over poor service is totally unnecessary and uncalled for. Regardless of the kind of service we receive, we always need to deliver the heart of gratitude and grace that God shows to us.

No matter what happens, always be thankful, for this is God's will for you who belong to Christ Jesus.
1 THESSALONIANS 5:18

November 23

A Generous Heart

*I*f you think that having a certain amount of money will make you feel secure, think again. That will never happen. The only way to reach that point of personal satisfaction is to have a generous heart, no matter how much or how little you have. If you cling to your possessions, they will never satisfy you. If you hold them loosely and share with others, you will always have enough.

Give generously to those in need, always being ready to share with others.
1 TIMOTHY 6:18

CONFRONTATION

*F*riends are quick to compliment each other, but confrontation comes much harder. In fact, many people will choose to avoid confronting a friend with an important issue. Do you have a Christian friend whose behavior blatantly defies what Jesus taught? Are you avoiding a confrontation with this friend? If so, pray about how to approach this subject with your friend. Remember to do it in love.

When Peter came to Antioch, I had to oppose him publicly, speaking strongly against what he was doing, for it was very wrong.
GALATIANS 2:11

GOD WILL BE WITH YOU

*S*ometimes it seems that your troubles begin the moment you trust God. The Bible says that troubles will come your way, and when they do, you need to use them as a way to grow closer to God. When God helps you through your problems, whether big or small, your joy increases in proportion to your faith. You know you can count on God whenever troubles come your way.

When your faith is tested, your endurance has a chance to grow.
JAMES 1:3

DISCOURAGEMENT

November 26

*W*hen you are discouraged, look at how God has been faithful to you in the past. Remember how He faithfully protected you and met your needs. Let God work in your life right now. Rely on Him for your strength and hope. Your reliance on God in tough times can be an example to others.

We are pressed on every side by troubles, but we are not crushed and broken. We are perplexed, but we don't give up and quit.
2 CORINTHIANS 4:8

November 27

THE ESSENCE OF LOYALTY

*N*ot all virtues require the same amount of effort. For example, patience takes a lot of work. By contrast, the virtue of loyalty requires little effort because it's the natural extension of love. When you defend the one you love from accusations and misunderstandings, you're being loyal. You know what God has done for you, but have you defended Him when others accuse Him?

"I will go wherever you go and live wherever you live. Your people will be my people, and your God will be my God."
RUTH 1:16

TAKE YOUR PLACE

*J*ust as every part of the human body plays a vital role in life, every Christian plays a vital role in the ministry of the church. God wants you to find your place in ministry. You won't be fulfilling God's plan for you if you don't. And your church will be incomplete without your involvement.

> *The human body has many parts, but the many parts make up only one body. So it is with the body of Christ. . . .*
> *This makes for harmony among the members, so that all the members care for each other equally.*
> I CORINTHIANS 12:12, 25

_____

_____

_____

_____

_____

RISE ABOVE

November 29

*T*o say that Jesus doesn't like mediocrity is an understatement. Nothing is more frustrating than watching someone with potential do nothing. Jesus offers a life beyond anything we can imagine, yet often we hang on to our mediocre existence like a beggar grasping a loaf of bread when a feast awaits. Jesus won't force Himself on you, but He wants you to turn from your indifference, rise above your mediocrity, and be sold out for Him.

> *"I advise you to buy gold from me—gold that has been purified by fire.*
> *Then you will be rich."*
> REVELATION 3:18

_____

_____

_____

_____

Not a Religion

*M*any people mistakenly believe that Christianity is a religion with a long list of dos and don'ts. Christianity is not a religion. At its heart, Christianity is just a relationship (between you and God with Christ providing the connection). There are no "rules" that you are required to follow to earn God's love, and there is no list of "don'ts" that would disqualify you from it.

Don't act thoughtlessly, but try to understand what the Lord wants you to do.
EPHESIANS 5:17

The Church Body Needs You

*T*he great thing about spiritual gifts is that everybody has at least one. The apostle Paul compares the church to a human body, which needs all of its parts to function. The next time you think the church doesn't need you, remember that you have a gift to give. Search the scriptures, pray, and ask your pastor to help you discover your spiritual gift.

Now there are different kinds of spiritual gifts, but it is the same Holy Spirit who is the source of them all.
1 CORINTHIANS 12:4

FRACTURED FAMILIES

*G*od knows about the family. After all, He invented it. God designed and intends the family to reflect His love. This attitude of love should exist between the husband and wife and between the parents and children. Your family may be fractured. You can begin a restoration process in your family by showing God's love.

So again I say, each man must love his wife as he loves himself, and the wife must respect her husband.
Children, obey your parents because you belong to the Lord, for this is the right thing to do.
EPHESIANS 5:33–6:1

CRITICISM TAKES NO EFFORT

*S*piritual gifts are designed by God to help the church. Why aspire to help, heal, teach, encourage, or serve others— when we can more easily criticize and find fault in others? After all, criticism comes more naturally for us. But it's what we do when we live by our old sin nature rather than by the power of the Holy Spirit—which requires a daily, willful surrender to God.

But if instead of showing love among yourselves you are always biting and
devouring one another, watch out! Beware of destroying one another.
GALATIANS 5:15

SYMPATHY

December 4

*T*ragedy in a friend's life can leave you speechless—not because you are shocked, but because you don't know what to say. So you say nothing. Don't let your momentary muteness prevent you from being a comfort to your friend. Is it possible to offer sympathy without saying anything? Sure. It may be enough for you to extend a hug or spend awhile sitting in silence with your friend. A lot can be said between friends when you don't say anything.

"Comfort, comfort my people," says your God.
ISAIAH 40:1

December 5

SEEKING GOD TAKES WORK

*N*othing worth seeking is easy to find. So why do we expend such little effort when we look for God? So many people look for God with a minimum of effort and then give up. They even conclude that God isn't there. Seeking and knowing God takes effort, time, and persistence. It also takes faith. If you seek God, you must believe that He will answer.

Anyone who wants to come to him must believe that there is a God and that he rewards those who sincerely seek him.
HEBREWS 11:6

God's Faithfulness

*F*ans of professional sports teams are fanatics for statistics. The statistics can give you an indication of how the player will perform in a future situation. However, we can think of only one example where the past record is a guarantee of future performance: God. You can rely on His record of past performance for the future. He is the same yesterday, today, and forever. You don't have to fear the future because you know what God has done in the past.

God has said, "I will never fail you. I will never forsake you."
HEBREWS 13:5

Teamwork

*I*n today's project-driven culture, you are wise to bring other people—with their diverse talents and gifts—into your projects. It's called teamwork. Whether you work in a business, a factory, a classroom, or a church, you need to recognize that teams—where people with complementary skills and passions work together for the good of the organization—are a must. This is no new concept. God has already said in His Word, "Now all of you together are Christ's body" (1 Corinthians 12:27).

We belong to each other, and each of us needs all the others.
ROMANS 12:5

WHO (OR WHAT) DO YOU LOVE?

*I*f your house were on fire and you had time to retrieve only one item, what would it be? Most likely, it would be the thing that has the most value to you. Many people proclaim to love God, but their actions don't support that proclamation. Their time, energy, and resources are devoted to other things. God isn't really important to them if they are able to ignore Him almost all of the time.

> *"Wherever your treasure is, there your heart and thoughts will also be."*
> MATTHEW 6:21

A PLACE FOR TOLERANCE

*W*hen you are tolerant toward others, you are patient with them even though their opinions or behavior may differ from yours. Permissiveness takes the person into account but focuses more on the behavior. Tolerance, on the other hand, respects and loves others while not necessarily endorsing their behavior. In fact, that characteristic is at the heart of tolerance, and this is what God asks you to do.

> *Don't you realize how kind, tolerant, and patient God is with you?*
> *Or don't you care?*
> ROMANS 2:4

Valuing Others

*I*t seems that our natural tendency is to be critical of other people. As with most of our natural tendencies and instincts, God wants us to act in the opposite manner. Think of it as a type of treasure hunt. You're looking for the value in people. You may be surprised that you find much more than you expected at the outset of your search.

Now all of you together are Christ's body, and each one of you is a separate and necessary part of it.
1 CORINTHIANS 12:27

Let the Children Come

*W*e must never forget that children are a gift from God. We are responsible to care for and nurture our children, and we must also teach them. No matter where you are in life, you need to be around children. Your own children are your first responsibility, but you should also invite the children of others to come to you. Give them your time, your teaching, and your love.

Then Jesus called for the children and said to the disciples,
"Let the children come to me. Don't stop them! For the Kingdom of God belongs to such as these."
LUKE 18:16

ANGER

*T*here are two kinds of anger. There is righteous anger that comes out of a godly response to sin. Righteous anger is not a reaction to a personal offense, and God always controls it. The second kind of anger is "personal anger." Losing your temper is personal anger. You say or do something you later regret. God is nowhere to be found in this type of anger. That's why the Bible warns against it. Don't let your personal anger take control of your life.

Stop your anger! Turn from your rage!
PSALM 37:8

_____

_____

_____

_____

_____

December 13

A TRUE FRIEND

*D*on't confuse casual friendship with true friendship. Even the friendliest person has only a few true friends, defined by honesty, loyalty, and sacrifice. A true friend possesses these qualities, whereas fair-weather friends disappear when you experience setbacks or don't give them what they need. With that in mind, we're going to tell you the name of your best friend. You already know Him, and He just happens to be our best friend, as well: His name is Jesus.

"I no longer call you servants.... Now you are my friends."
JOHN 15:15

_____

_____

_____

_____

_____

Time for a Heart Exam

"The devil made me do it." The devil doesn't make you do anything. Your heart does. The heart of every person is inclined toward sin from the moment of birth. It doesn't get any better on its own. A heart transplant is required if you are going to enjoy real life. Your sinful heart must be replaced with a heart filled with God's love.

> *"The human heart is most deceitful and desperately wicked.*
> *Who really knows how bad it is?"*
> JEREMIAH 17:9

Seek Wisdom

No matter where you look, there's opportunity. Opportunity is plentiful and cheap. What you need is wisdom in order to sort through the opportunities. Wisdom leads to good judgment, which enables you to make good decisions. And if you're able to make good decisions, you will have the ability to sort through the worthwhile opportunities that come your way.

> *How wonderful to be wise, to be able to analyze and interpret things.*
> ECCLESIASTES 8:1

GOD'S NEW MATH

December 16

In normal arithmetic, if you give something away, you end up with less than you started out with. But in God's math, if you give something to Him, you end up with more than you started out with. What you get in return will be in spiritual blessings. His blessings (in whatever form) are always more valuable than what you've given away.

"I will open the windows of heaven for you. I will pour out a blessing so great you won't have enough room to take it in! Try it! Let me prove it to you!"
MALACHI 3:10

December 17

STOP JUDGING

Have you ever exaggerated the faults of others while excusing or ignoring your own? That's why the story of the woman caught in adultery has a universal application. The teachers demanded an answer, so Jesus stood up and said, "All right, stone her. But let those who have never sinned throw the first stones!" The next time we feel compelled to judge someone, we need to remember what Jesus said.

"Let those who have never sinned throw the first stones!"
JOHN 8:7

A Pure Heart

*W*hen we realize and act on the fact that Jesus has freed us from a "life that is dominated by sin" (Romans 7:24), we are free to follow our "heart's desires" (Psalm 37:4). When our hearts are pure, God will fill them with His desires and prompt us to do what He wants us to do, "for God is greater than our hearts" (1 John 3:20).

Take delight in the LORD, and he will give you your heart's desires.
PSALM 37:4

Inside Out

*T*he heart is one of the world's most powerful images. God promises to give you the desires of your heart (Psalm 37:4), as long as your desires are in line with His. But wait. There's a catch. You don't have a pure heart, and neither do we. The prophet Jeremiah wrote, "The human heart is most deceitful and desperately wicked" (Jeremiah 17:9). That's why God asks us to believe in our hearts and to invite Him in. He wants to change us from the inside out.

"I, the LORD, search all hearts and examine secret motives."
JEREMIAH 17:10

GOD'S WEB

God works on many levels every single day of your life. He is present in your casual relationships, prompting you to see others through His eyes of love and compassion. He gives you strength when the pressure mounts at work or at school. God shows Himself through the interactions with those you care about most. It's as if God is weaving a huge web composed of the small stuff He is doing in everyone's lives.

Search for the LORD and for his strength, and keep on searching.
1 CHRONICLES 16:11

WHAT NOT TO LOOK AT

If you are looking for faults in someone else, you are sure to find them. Focusing on the deficiencies of someone else will cause you to think less of that person (and more of yourself). You'll find it hard to cooperate with that person, and you're likely to be critical. God wants you to be patient with them and assist them in the areas of their weakness.

Be humble and gentle. Be patient with each other, making allowance
for each other's faults because of your love.
EPHESIANS 4:2

LIVING LETTERS

*G*od is very deliberate about the relationships He puts you in. What you say is important. But don't overemphasize your words at the expense of your life. The truth is that the people you meet are more likely to see Christ in your actions than in your words. Paul compared the life of a Christian to a "living letter," meaning that your life is like a "letter of recommendation," written in the hearts of others.

Your lives are a letter written in our hearts, and everyone can read it
and recognize our good work among you.
2 CORINTHIANS 3:2

READY AND WILLING

*E*ver since Jesus left the earth nearly two thousand years ago, people have been predicting when the world is going to end. The important thing is to be sure of these two things: Are you ready for the Lord's return? And are you living your life fully each day until Christ comes back or you die, whichever occurs first?

"However, no one knows the day or the hour when these things will happen."
MATTHEW 24:36

LIFE AFTER DEATH

Through God's Word, we have assurance of life after death. The Christian's new body will be indestructible and immune from all defects. Jesus gave His followers a glimpse of what was coming when He raised His friend Lazarus from the dead (John 11:17–44). The same power that Jesus used to transform the dead body of Lazarus is the same power God will use to transform our bodies.

Let me tell you a wonderful secret God has revealed to us.
Not all of us will die, but we will all be transformed.
1 CORINTHIANS 15:51

GOD'S GIFT TO YOU

Many people never realize the real meaning of God's Christmas gift—His Son, Jesus. They keep Him wrapped in a religious package and then set Him on a shelf in their lives. They never take Him out of the box and have a real relationship with Him. Please don't make the tragic mistake of keeping Jesus under the wrapping. Enjoy the full benefit of Him by getting to know Him personally and intimately.

"The Savior—yes, the Messiah, the Lord—has been born tonight in Bethlehem, the city of David!"
LUKE 2:11

THE PUREST OF THE PURE

*W*hen we run across a verse that says, "You must be holy in everything you do, just as God—who chose you to be his children—is holy" (1 Peter 1:15)—well, that's tough to understand. The only way for us to be holy is for God to see Jesus—the purest of the pure—in our lives.

You know that God paid a ransom to save you. . .with the precious lifeblood of Christ, the sinless, spotless Lamb of God. God chose him for this purpose.
1 PETER 1:18–20

_____

_____

_____

_____

_____

REAL HOPE

*W*e put our hope in God, that what He says in His Word is true. And we put our hope in Jesus, that what He did on the cross counts for us. This is real hope, the kind that enables us to live for God now while we look forward to living with Him in the future.

We should live in this evil world with self-control, right conduct, and devotion to God, while we look forward to that wonderful event when the glory of our great God and Savior, Jesus Christ, will be revealed.
TITUS 2:12–13

_____

_____

_____

_____

_____

OBEDIENCE MATTERS

December 28

*L*iving life so God sees Jesus in us requires something of us: obedience. God didn't force you to accept Jesus, and He's not going to force you to live like Jesus. He wants us to look at each situation we encounter and ask, "What would Jesus do?"

Follow God's example in everything you do, because you are his dear children. Live a life filled with love for others, following the example of Christ, who loved you and gave himself as a sacrifice to take away your sins.
EPHESIANS 5:1–2

_____

_____

_____

_____

_____

December 29

WHEN GOD'S PATIENCE RUNS OUT

*T*he Bible says, "The Lord isn't really being slow about his promise to return, as some people think. No, he is being patient for your sake" (2 Peter 3:9). When you have patience, you wait for the right moment. We believe that God is waiting for the right moment to send Jesus back to earth. And that moment has a lot to do with people giving God their hearts.

That is why the LORD says, "Turn to me now, while there is time! Give me your hearts."
JOEL 2:12

_____

_____

_____

_____

_____

THE SECOND COMING

The New Testament begins with the historical record of the first coming of Jesus to earth. The Bible ends with the fact that Jesus, God in the flesh, will return someday. Jesus came as a Savior the first time. When He comes again, He will be coming to reward and repay according to what people have done. All those who have accepted God's plan of salvation through Jesus will receive the wonderful reward of eternal life in heaven. Those who have refused will receive the judgment they deserve.

"Yes, I am coming soon!"
REVELATION 22:20

_____

_____

_____

_____

_____

TAKE A GOOD LOOK

If you've never studied astronomy, you could look at the stars all night long and never know anything about them. However, if you were to get a star chart and a telescope, those little points of light would take on more meaning and significance. It's the same with the places where God is working in your life. If you don't make an effort to know God, you'll miss out on the amazing things God is doing now and wants to do in the future.

May grace and peace be yours from God our Father and from the Lord Jesus Christ.
GALATIANS 1:3

_____

_____

_____

_____

_____

INDEX